To the Heart of the Mystery of the Redemption

HANS URS VON BALTHASAR
ADRIENNE VON SPEYR

To the Heart of the Mystery of the Redemption

Preface by Cardinal Henri de Lubac (1980)
Postscript by Jacques Servais, S.J. (2005)

TRANSLATED BY ANNE ENGLUND NASH

IGNATIUS PRESS   SAN FRANCISCO

Title of the French original:
Au coeur du mystère rédempteur
Second edition, © 2005 by SOCÉVAL Éditions,
Magny-les-Hameaux (France)

Cover art:
Crucifixion; Descent from the Cross
From the Psalter of Ingeburg of
Denmark, Queen of France. Ca. 1210 CE.
30 x 20 cm. Ms.9, folio 27 recto.
Photo: René-Gabriel Ojéda.
© Réunion des Musées Nationaux /
Art Resource, New York

Cover design by Roxanne Mei Lum

Contents

III. *Adrienne von Speyr*
FLASHES OF THE PASSION

Jacques Servais, S.J.
POSTSCRIPT

FOREWORD

The centenary of the birth of Father Hans Urs von Balthasar prompts us to republish two conferences that the Swiss theologian gave before an audience composed essentially of young Parisian priests in the midst of the sixties, in that turbulent and at times obscure postconciliar period. It is a lantern in the hand that von Balthasar advances in the midst of the turmoil, the lantern of the Word, unchanged and ever new, judge of the present and criterion for the future. Two themes are treated, but it is a question of essentially the same subject considered from two perspectives: on the one hand, Christ the Redeemer, nailed to the wood of the Cross, his arms opened to the world he is redeeming; on the other, Mary, and with her the Church, who consents to the sacrifice of her Lord and welcomes, in silence, the new Life. It is indeed to the heart of the mystery of redemption that Father von Balthasar leads us, in order, finally, to yield the floor to one of those who participated with all their being in this mystery, Adrienne von Speyr.

Two conferences, then, held for the study days of the priestly association Lumen Gentium[1] and published a first time in the French journal *Communio*,[2] then a second time,

---

[1] 81, rue Madame, Paris 6e.

[2] Vol. 2, no. 3 (May 1977): 36–42. Father von Balthasar published these extracts as an addition to his article on the same subject, entitled "Fragments sur la Croix trinitaire" (Fragments on the trinitarian Cross), pp. 24–35.

in 1980,[3] in a little volume containing as well an anthology of meditations by Adrienne von Speyr on the Passion, selected by Father von Balthasar, her confessor and editor.[4] It is to Father Henri de Lubac, S.J., that we owe the fortuitous initiative of having brought together these three contributions, which are different in nature, to be sure, but intimately linked with each other, as he himself suggests in his preface.[5] The present work reproduces this edition in its entirety,[6] now expanded with a postscript that we hope will help the young reader of the new millennium to inherit the wealth bequeathed by Father von Balthasar.

JACQUES SERVAIS, S.J.

[3] The work constitutes the first volume of the series Sentiers de Lumière, published by the C.L.D.

[4] Translated from German to French by G. Chantraine and R. Brague, revised for the present edition by I. Crahay.

[5] We have provided Father de Lubac's preface with a few notes updating and completing the information that the latter gave at that time.

[6] The original text of the two conferences by Father von Balthasar is in French. We have taken the liberty of updating some of the notes from this text through reference to particular existing French translations and of making slight alterations in some expressions used by the participants in the "Replies to the Questions of Priests", the discussion that followed each of these conferences.

Henri de Lubac

Preface of 1980

Saint Paul is the first witness of our faith. Overwhelmed by Christ, immediately incorporated into the nascent Church, he was taught by her. As personal as his experience had been, as unique and as decisive as was the mission with which he was invested (we know with what vehemence he could claim it), it was the unique faith of this Church that he handed on. He was aware of this, and when necessary he said so explicitly: he gave to his communities what he himself had received. So it is for the Resurrection; so it is for the Eucharist. So it is, at the same time, for the meaning of the Cross, where our redemption is carried out.

Christ, says Paul, "died for all"; each one can say: "He was handed over for me"; "in him God reconciled the world to himself." Paul also recalls that, on the night when he was going to be handed over, the Lord Jesus said: "Here is my body (which will be handed over) for you." In the three Synoptic Gospels, in the account of that Supper, it is said in parallel ways that the blood of Jesus will be poured out "for you and for many". And this is what the priest, speaking in the name of Christ, says two times, of the Body and of the Blood, at the moment of the Consecration in each eucharistic celebration.

"The nucleus and organizational center of the Christian faith" consists in this affirmation. This shows the importance of the subject treated in this little volume. Rightly persuaded that Christianity remains unintelligible and that all explanations and justifications are useless as long as it is presented, so to speak, in detached pieces, Father Hans Urs von Balthasar has long been concerned with an energetic "return to the center".[1] He wants to make visible, according to the title of one of his books, "the whole in the fragment"[2]—in each fragment; and increasingly he is striving, in his immense work, to consolidate all the aspects of the one Mystery more strongly by showing their convergence in the paradox—let us say with Paul, the scandal—of the Cross of Jesus.

Such is the fundamental intention of that "ecclesial drama" which he is in the process of constructing—the first three volumes of it have been published to date[3]—and to which the five volumes of the *Glory of the Lord* served, so to speak, as a portico.[4] Such is more precisely the object of the pages that are about to be read. Their author deliberately wanted to confine himself to a simple, objective, precise presentation in what might be called a catechetical format. Starting with the concrete facts from the New Testament, he proposes various explanations gathered from the theological tradition. Each of them has its role to play in leading us,

[1] *Einfaltungen: Auf Wegen christlicher Einigung*, 1969.

[2] *A Theological Anthropology* (New York: Sheed and Ward, 1967) (original German: *Das Ganze im Fragment: Aspekte der Geschichtstheologie*, 1963).

[3] The four volumes (in five) have since appeared: *Theo-Drama: Theological Dramatic Theory* (San Francisco: Ignatius Press, 1988–1998) (original German: *Theodramatik*, 1973–1983).

[4] *The Glory of the Lord: A Theological Aesthetics*, 7 vols. (San Francisco: Ignatius Press; New York: Crossroad, 1982–1989) (original German: *Herrlichkeit: Eine theologische Ästhetik*, 1961–1969). The trilogy was completed by the publication of *Theo-logic*, 3 vols. (San Francisco: Ignatius Press, 2000–2005) (original German: *Theologik*, 1985–1987), and the final *Epilogue* (San Francisco: Ignatius Press, 2004) (original German: *Epilog*, 1987).

by approaching it from different angles, to grasp as well as possible what is always an ineffable mystery.

The second part offers us a major example of that comprehensive unity in which each of the statements that contribute to the Catholic synthesis must be viewed. Our traditional piety toward the Virgin Mary has often been poorly understood (and this was not always solely by outside observers). When it appeared more or less as a kind of parallel cult, it was entirely distorted. But the remedy was not in banishing it or at least relegating it to the shadows. Brought back into the light of the total Mystery, the mystery of Mary is clarified, is justified, or rather, is seen to be essential. It is of this that Father von Balthasar, faithful to the orientation recalled by Vatican II in the final chapter of its Dogmatic Constitution on the Church, provides us with a new perception by having us meditate on the role of Mary, as a figure and archetype of the Church, in the work of the one Redeemer.[5] The reflections that he proposes to us will contribute to a deepening of our faith.

But faith can never remain pure light. Every living member of the Church is called to enter into her profound sentiments, which are those of Mary at the foot of the Cross. Now there is no better initiation into this mystery than the experience received from the mystics, who are no more lacking to the present generation than to earlier ones. This is why we have placed, in the third part, several carefully chosen meditations on the Passion from Adrienne von Speyr,

[5] See on this subject the contribution of Hans Urs von Balthasar to the volume, published in collaboration with Joseph Ratzinger, entitled *Mary: The Church at the Source*, trans. Adrian Walker (San Francisco: Ignatius Press, 2005), particularly pp. 9–10, 125–41 (original German: *Maria: Kirche im Ursprung*, 1997).

whose testimony was cited by Father von Balthasar, editor of her writings.[6] They will introduce the reader into that participation in the mystery of the redemption which the first two parts of the work present.

CARDINAL HENRI DE LUBAC, S.J. (1896–1991)

[6] As Father von Balthasar has urged us, we hope to encourage the discovery of Adrienne von Speyr by the English reader through some of the following works: Adrienne von Speyr, *The World of Prayer*, with a foreword by Hans Urs von Balthasar, trans. Graham Harrison (San Francisco: Ignatius Press, 1985); *Handmaid of the Lord*, trans. E. A. Nelson (San Francisco: Ignatius Press, 1985); and *The Cross, Word and Sacrament*, trans. Graham Harrison (San Francisco: Ignatius Press, 1983). As an introduction to her life, work, and spiritual journey, the reader should consult Hans Urs von Balthasar, *First Glance at Adrienne von Speyr*, trans. Antje Lawry and Sr. Sergia Englund, O.C.D. (San Francisco: Ignatius Press, 1981). Ignatius Press continues to publish the works of Adrienne von Speyr in English translation, most recently: *The Book of All Saints*, vol. 1, trans. David Schindler, Jr. (2008); *The Boundless God*, trans. Helena M. Tomko (2004); *Light and Images: Elements of Contemplation*, trans. David Schindler, Jr. (2004); *Lumina and New Lumina*, trans. Adrian Walker (2008).

I

Hans Urs von Balthasar

CHRIST THE REDEEMER

INTRODUCTION

All over the world, the best young people are seeking God. They would like to discover the paths where they can meet him, where they can experience him, where they can be challenged by him. They are tired of sociological and psychological expedients, of all the banal substitutes for the truly miraculous.

In order to respond to their desire—which corresponds, moreover, to that of true Christians of all ages—let us not delay: let us be spiritual men who live and know how to hand on the extraordinary mystery that is at the center of our faith, the mystery without which all Christianity becomes trivial and, thereby, ineffective.

At the center of our faith: the Cross

"For I decided to know nothing among you except Jesus Christ and him crucified" (1 Cor 2:2): there you have Paul's plan of action. Why? Because the entire Credo of the early Church was focused on the interpretation of the appalling end of Jesus, of the Cross, as having been brought about *pro nobis*, for us; Paul even says: for each one of us, thus, *for me*.

"The life I now live in the flesh I live by faith in the Son of God, who loved me and gave himself for me" (Gal 2:20).

What effect can such an act of love have? Is it a manifestation of solidarity? But if I suffer from cancer, what good does it do me if someone else lets himself be stricken by the same illness in order to keep me company? In order to understand the original faith, we must certainly go beyond the simple concept of solidarity.

For the early Church, this "going beyond" was justified after the experience of the Resurrection. Far from being a private event in the history of Jesus, it is the attestation on God's part that this crucified Jesus is truly the advent of the kingdom of God, of the pardon of faults, of the justification of the sinner, of filial adoption.

Well, then, what did happen on the Cross?

The ancient Roman liturgy speaks of a *sacrum commercium*, or *admirabile commercium*, of a mysterious exchange that Saint Paul expresses by these words: "[If] one has died for all, therefore all have died" (2 Cor 5:13), which obviously means: if a single one has the competence and the authorization to die for all, that creates an objective fact that affects them all. Consequently, Paul can continue: "And he died for all, that those who live might live no longer for themselves but for him who for their sake died and was raised" (2 Cor 5:15).

Four aspects of the mystery

Here we are before a mystery that is usually referred to as redemption. Let us not dwell on questions of terminology. It is clear that, if this Christian mystery is a reality, it is absolutely unique. Consequently, no concept drawn from common experience will be able to exhaust it.

This is what Saint Thomas has demonstrated superlatively in his Christology by aligning four concepts that all capture one aspect of the mystery but that all also need to be surpassed and that are all mutually complementary. Here they

are, all indispensable, each by itself insufficient: merit, sat- —
isfaction, sacrifice, redemption (or atonement).

We will come back to this. Let us say briefly in advance
that all have their references in Scripture, in the Fathers, and
in the great theologians. Scripture seems to advocate sacrificial vocabulary (Letter to the Hebrews); the Fathers, atone-
ment/redemption; Saint Anselm, satisfaction; Saint Thomas,
merit, while stressing the interpenetration of the four aspects.

The shortcomings are also immediately apparent:

—*Sacrifice* comes from the Old Testament and nonbiblical religions; now Christ, at once priest and victim, transcends
this stage of relations with God.

— *Atonement/redemption* is a vivid image; but from whom would
Christ be redeeming us? Not from the devil, who cannot
have true rights over sinners; not from God the Father and
his justice or his anger, since it is precisely the Father who
in his love for the world has handed over his Son to us.

— *Satisfaction*: in one sense, yes: for us who are incapable of reconciling ourselves with God, Christ effectively works this
reconciliation, and Scripture instills in us the idea that at the
Cross it was not merely a question of a symbol by which
God demonstrated that he was already reconciled. But what
event in this world could influence God? Change his attitude
toward the world? That seems metaphysically impossible.

— Finally, *merit*, supereminently: because, according to Anselm
and Thomas, the person who suffers is divine and since he is
through his Incarnation the Head of the Body of mankind.
But is this *merit* enough to account for the *exchange* between
Christ and us?

It thus seems that none of the concepts exhausts the mystery. And that is just what we would have to expect.

~

How, then, shall we proceed?

1. First of all, we are going to say a word about the relation in the Gospel between the earthly Jesus going to his death and the risen Christ as he appears in the faith of the early Christians.

2. It will then be necessary to confront the formidable problem—evangelical and theological at the same time—of the relation between the wrath of God (*orgē*) and his mercy, in other words, the problem of the beloved Son handed over to sinners by God the Father.

3. Finally, a word about the theories of redemption, in particular that of Anselm, which was the classic one until thirty years ago but nearly unanimously abandoned since.

And as a final word, we will make a very brief reflection on the possibility of proclaiming the mystery of the Cross today.

I

JESUS BEFORE AND AFTER THE CROSS

The Jesus of history and the Christ of faith

With the progress of exegetical works, the abyss between the *Jesus of history* and the *Christ of faith* seems to grow ever greater. Many of the words and actions of Jesus that used to seem to us to reveal his consciousness as redeemer are today suspected of being post-Paschal interpretations. Could Christ have referred to himself as the *lytron* (ransom) for the multitude?

I would be inclined to side with Father Léon-Dufour when he said: "Jesus never theorized about himself; he did not want to lock himself into a title, whatever it might be. So is it good form to attribute to Jesus words that would make him a theoretician of his existence?"[1]

The authenticity of the announcements of the Passion is disputed. Usually, however, there is agreement about keeping an authentic kernel, perhaps represented by a passage such as Mark 8:31: "The Son of man must suffer many things and be rejected."

The long list of indirect predictions drawn up by J. Jeremias has also been decimated.

The *Source* (Q), it is said, contains nothing; but Schürmann has pointed out that nothing could have been expected of it, since its intention was only to gather together the doctrinal *logia* of Jesus.

---

[1] X. Léon-Dufour, A. Vergote, R. Bureau, and J. Moingt, *Mort pour nos péchés* (Brussels, 1976), p. 37.

— The big question remains the following: Did Jesus know in advance that his death was included in his vocation? And if he did, that this death was salvific for the entire world?

Bultmann categorically denies that we could know what meaning Jesus gave his death. His disciples retraced his steps: they understand that a post-Paschal faith would be vain without some solid link between the *Christ of faith* and Jesus of Nazareth; the most critical and fastidious Catholic exegetes (like A. Vögtle and R. Pesch) admit at least that the consciousness Jesus had of his person and his mission differs essentially from that of all the prophets and even of the Baptist.

Jesus does not present himself solely as the precursor and proclaimer of the kingdom of God; he declares that this kingdom has begun with his presence, that its full coming is near, so near that some will be present at its arrival (Mk 9:1), and that the attitude a man takes toward him decides the eternal fate of that man (Mk 8:38). More and more we recognize that, with Jesus, this expectation of the kingdom and of the end of history differs completely from the apocalyptic expectations of contemporary Judaism. It is obvious, on the other hand, that Jesus' whole attitude was an open provocation to official Judaism—he made himself judge of the Torah, which amounted to attributing a divine authority to himself—so that he had to allow for the probability of a violent death. His words and his actions placed his life at stake.

Did Jesus conceive of his death and the coming of the kingdom as interlocked?

Were the Gospels wrong, then, in presenting Jesus' imminent death and the coming of the kingdom, that is, the great pardon of the Father for the sin of the world, the descent of the divine Spirit into hearts, as coinciding in Jesus' consciousness—while leaving to the early Church the task and secondary concern of distinguishing between Resurrection and final Parousia?

For Jesus himself, in his primary conception, the two are mixed together: with his own end he attains not only the goal of his personal mission but the end of the world—then, the Gospels explain, he must carry the sin of the entire world and (in a true sense) overcome it.

It seems to me that here we must listen to J. Moltmann,[2] who wants to instill in exegetes the idea that the existence of Jesus of Nazareth was a highly theological phenomenon, unique in Israel's whole history of salvation. His death, consequently, had also to be an unparalleled theological event for which it is vain to seek purely external causes—hatred of the Jews, the fear of Pilate. The central fact is the extraordinary scandal that the *Abba*, on whom Jesus had founded his entire existence, abandoned him on the Cross, where he died with the great cry of distress reported by Mark (15:34, 37) and Matthew (27:46, 50), so unbearable that it was later softened by Luke (23:46) and John (19:30).

And can one really deny that the fundamental outline of the Synoptics has a historical foundation, that is, that Jesus, after a turning point in his active life, begins to go up to Jerusalem, his face set: *faciem suam firmavit*? Can it be denied that he spoke of his *hour*, of the hour that he was awaiting, that had not yet arrived, that would be at once the hour of the Father and that of shadows?

Did he know what this hour had in store for him? Yes and no.

No, because it is essential to the obedience of Jesus toward his message to anticipate nothing. The hour belongs to the Father; no one knows it, neither men nor angels nor the Son. K. Rahner is very right to remind theologians who

---

[2] Jürgen Moltmann, *Der gekreuzigte Gott* (Munich, 1972), pp. 121–46.

insist on the omniscience of Christ that at certain moments it is much more perfect to obey without knowing than to master the situation through his knowledge.

Yes, nonetheless: Jesus knows at least that *the hour* will contain what is essential, the dénouement of his tragic failure with respect to Israel. But at what a price! That of the fulfillment of the prophecies about the Servant of Yahweh:

You, who say: "I have spent my strength for nothing", "I will give you as a light to the nations, that my salvation may reach to the end of the earth" (Is 49:4, 6).

Beyond human strength, through the imposition of an incalculable and excessive burden, God will accomplish through him what he, as man, could never have gone through. Is this not already the Pauline formula: "[It was God who] in Christ was reconciling the world to himself" (2 Cor 5:19).

That this was not achieved without Jesus being conscious of it is testified to by the oblation he makes of himself in the Eucharist at the Last Supper. Although God disposes of Jesus in the Passion and at the hour of abandonment, Jesus himself also disposes of himself by giving his effective assent in advance to all that his Father will do with him.

I close this much too rapid sketch about Jesus with an assertion that might seem to have been formulated a priori, but that seems to me to contain a sine qua non condition for all coherent Christian faith: it would be impossible for the soteriological statements of the early Church, developed by Paul and John, to give an objective interpretation of the Cross—and of the whole existence of Jesus—if Jesus himself had not been conscious of the universal meaning of his mission: the reconciliation of the world with God.

2

THE BELOVED SON
HANDED OVER BY THE FATHER

Let us pass on to the second point: Why this method of redemption? Was it really necessary for a victim to appease the wrath of God?

The "wrath" of God and his love

The question is embarrassing, since, on the one hand, the New Testament, like the Old, speaks abundantly of the wrath of God. To give just three examples:

— "much more shall we be saved by [Christ] from the wrath of God (salvi erimus ab ira per ipsum)" (Rom 5:9);

— the Son coming from heaven "delivers us from the wrath to come (qui erip[u]it nos ab ira ventura)" (1 Thess 1:10); as for the Jews, "God's wrath has come upon them at last!" (1 Thess 2:16);

— finally, the Apocalypse will even speak of "the wrath of the Lamb (*orgē tou arniou*)" (Rev 6:16) and of the "great day of their wrath" (that of God and of the Lamb) (Rev 6:17).

On the other hand, we have passages where the entire initiative of reconciliation comes from a God who is Love:

— "God so loved the world that he gave his only-begotten Son" (Jn 3:16);

— "He who did not spare his own Son . . . will he not also give us all things with him?" (Rom 8:32);

— Through the work of the Cross, he demonstrated to us his efficacious will for reconciliation (cf. 2 Cor 5:19).

And did not Christ himself always proclaim in parables and action this disposition of the Father—for example, in the story of the prodigal son (Lk 15:11–32)?

There must be some way to reconcile these apparently contradictory statements. In God, wrath is not a passion; it is the total reprobation of sin, which contradicts the divine goodness; and it can be said that God, in loving sinful man, hates the sin and condemns it. But that detested sin is found precisely in the beloved man: it is he who has committed it. It was thus necessary to be able to find a method to separate the sin from the sinner—and it is of this that the Pauline texts speak to us, whether we like their mystical realism or not.

Christ burdened with sin

In reality, it is a question of a gathering together, a concentration of universal sin in Christ: "[God] made him to be sin who knew no sin, so that in him we might become the righteousness of God" (2 Cor 5:21).

Two things must be noted here: on the one hand, "righteousness [or justice] of God" always designates, according to the Old Testament, the salvific justice of the Covenant, and "justice" in Saint Paul never has a vindictive sense; on the other hand, Christ can be made "sin" (not "sinner") precisely because he is without sin.

A similar assertion is formulated in Galatians 3:13: "Christ redeemed us . . . , having become a curse for us—for it is written, 'Cursed be every one who hangs on a tree.'" We find here again that "for us", that exchange of place, which is at the center of all New Testament soteriology.

The same basic assertion is found again in Romans 8:3: "Sending his own Son in the likeness of sinful flesh and for sin, [God] condemned sin in the flesh."

The same idea is developed in the long passage of Ephesians 2, where it is said that "through the cross", Christ "in himself" brought "hostility to an end".

Let us recall once again that if God *hands over* his Son to this process of exchange, it is also said that Christ hands himself over, and not only through obedience, but through love: "The life I now live in the flesh I live by faith in the Son of God, who loved me and gave himself for me" (Gal 2:20).

John speaks much the same way in the discourse following the Last Supper.

Christ dead and risen "for all"

Paul's assertion ends logically in observing the success of this exchange, which the liturgy, as we have said, would very early on call the *sacrum commercium* or the *admirabile commercium*.[1]

The Pauline affirmation is solemn, realistic, precise, in no way rhetorical: "We are convinced that one has died for all; therefore all have died. And he died for all, that those who live might live no longer for themselves but for him who for their sake died and was raised" (2 Cor 5:14–15).

Once again, "for us", "for them" is said: which implies a person capable of that substitution—some man might well

[1] Martin Herz, *Sacrum Commercium* (Munich, 1958).

die for another or for a good cause, but never for all and in such a way that all participate in his death and, thereby, in his Resurrection. It is matter here of uprooting men from their own land in order to have them take root elsewhere, of transplanting them, as Colossians 1:13 says. It cannot, thus, be a question of interpreting this event as a purely juridical transfer, as Father Duquoc seems to do in speaking of the theory of satisfaction.[2] The transplantation in question is real; it sets up a new ontology of man, henceforth incorporated "into the kingdom of the beloved Son". Why should we be "so allergic to this game of compensation"? as Duquoc says, who would like to interpret the soteriological dynamism of the New Testament as the dynamism of man's history of liberation.[3]

Let us content ourselves with these texts, leaving aside the question of a more intimate association of the faithful with this death and this Resurrection of Christ through baptism and the Eucharist, such as Romans 6 and 1 Corinthians 10 and 11 describe it.

Anyone who would wish to take these texts for what they mean should in any case admit one fact: the substitution that Paul describes cannot be understood as a pure symbol by which God would supposedly demonstrate the intensity and seriousness of his love or would indicate to us that in truth there is no wrath in him. Paul presents an event, not a symbol, and an event by which, as he expressly says, God reconciles the world to himself.

If we compare Saint John's meditation on this event, we arrive at the same conclusion. The Good Shepherd gives his

---

[2] *Christologie: Essai dogmatique*, vol. 2, *Le Messie* (Paris, 1972), pp. 200, 213ff.

[3] Ibid., pp. 214–16.

life for his sheep, and he gives it of his own accord so as to obtain eternal life for them (10:17ff.); and when he is lifted up from the earth, he will draw all men to himself (12:32); he himself will do it, and not God alone, showing us in the Crucified a symbol of his love.

3

THEORIES OF THE REDEMPTION

Let us turn the floor over now to the theologians, so that they may explain to us, if they can, what is presented to us by revelation. We have tried to feel the specific weight of it; the explanations they are going to give us should neither reduce it nor make it vanish into thin air.

EXPLANATIONS TO BE ELIMINATED

Certain conceptions, it seems to me, can be eliminated straightaway.

Might the Pauline texts have only a relative value?

It is not possible to dismiss the Pauline texts quoted, or other similar passages, as witnesses of a *later* New Testament soteriology,[1] one that could consequently be relativized.

Of course, the mystery presents several aspects, and we will never succeed in making a perfect synthesis of them. Nevertheless, not only are the Pauline epistles the most ancient documents that we possess; not only do they incorporate and develop soteriological formulas that are still older; but the earliest Credo, the one quoted to us by Paul in 1 Corinthians 15, already contains the formula *pro nobis*,[2]

---

[1] K. Rahner and, in practically the same sense, Father Duquoc.
[2] 1 Cor 15:3: "for our sins"; cf. 15:11: "and so you have believed."

and it was starting from this that the whole Credo was going to develop: "Propter nos homines et propter nostram salutem . . . crucifixus etiam pro nobis" (for us men and for our salvation . . . for our sake he was crucified).

Martin Hengel,[3] moreover, has demonstrated, in a memorable study, that all the theories, Bultmann's as well as others, that assign very distinct stages to an evolution of Christology (a Palestinian phase, then a transition to Hellenistic Judaism, and finally a purely Hellenistic phase of pagan origin) do not take into account the brevity of the time in question: according to Hengel, in the very first years after the death of Christ, more things took place in Christology than in all future centuries.

Might pro nobis *signify merely a human solidarity?*

The early *pro nobis* was meant to express more than an action in our favor, something other than a gesture of solidarity for the benefit of men.

Of course, Christ crucified is in solidarity with us sinners: the two thieves show this well enough. But, once again, what good with this solidarity do us if it did not have the potential of being intensified into a true substitution?

Here I cannot agree completely with the excellent reflections of Father Moingt on the redemptive death of the Lord. He wishes to take into consideration the "substitutive value of this death, for it is linked to the 'representative' character of Christ", but he, like a number of theologians today, excludes the supposition that "Christ offered himself with the idea that reparation was due for our sins." In fact, he

---

[3] "Christologie und neutestamentliche Chronologie", in *Neues Testament und Geschichte* (Tübingen, 1972), pp. 43–67.

says, "for the Bible, redemption is the privilege of the divine sovereignty; no human offering has of itself the value of an expiation for others . . . no offering is commensurate either to the offense that sin has given to God or to the grace that he grants."[4]

It is therefore necessary, Father Moingt concludes, to avoid at all costs speaking "in terms of an exchange",[5] that is, to avoid Anselmian theology and to keep to the idea of a "solidarity" having an efficacious significance for us: "The invasion of the Spirit into mankind . . . was made possible by the fact that a man, invested by God with a universal mission, annihilated himself totally in the total Yes to God. . . . Thanks to his solidarity with us, we all have solidarity with his faith, which can henceforth overcome the human incredulity in each of us."[6]

Might not Jesus be simply a privileged man?

We find ourselves now on a level with a great number of modern Christologies, which can have notable differences between them, from those that are of a very free conception (Küng and probably Schillebeeckx) up to nearly traditional systems (like Galot), whose most outstanding representative is without doubt Karl Rahner.

Let us turn our attention to the position of the latter, which can be summed up in three assertions:

a. It is impossible for a second cause to be able to influence God and make him change his mind. The idea of a

---

[4] In Léon-Dufour et al., *Mort pour nos péchés*.
[5] Ibid., p. 150.
[6] Ibid., p. 155.

sacrifice that could appease an angry divinity was current among the ancients (pagan and Jewish) but is not really still accessible to us. God himself is the initiator of the reconciliation.

b. Jesus is the bearer of the divine promise concerning an ultimate and universal reconciliation; he is aware of it, and in his death he achieves his mission of incarnating that commitment of God to the end, the freely accepted death being the final and decisive act of a fully human and religious life.

c. We could thus say that this death on the Cross, which recapitulates a life that proclaims God's commitment, possesses "a causality of a quasi-sacramental and real-symbolic [*realsymbolisch*] nature. In this causality what is signified, in this case God's salvific will, posits the sign, in this case the death of Jesus along with his resurrection, and in and through the sign it causes what is signified."[7]

Personally, I do not see the essential difference between this position and those of Küng,[8] Schillebeeckx,[9] and perhaps also Father Moingt: Jesus is a privileged man by virtue of his unique relation to God, whom he calls Father, and endowed with a universal mission of proclaiming salvation.

But we can also perhaps reduce to this position the soteriology of Father Galot,[10] based on the notion of the Covenant. This Covenant is, from the beginning, a free initiative of God; it is consummated in the obedient response

---

[7] *Foundations of Christian Faith*, trans. William V. Dych (New York: Crossroad, 1984), p. 284. Cf. "Der eine Jesus Christus und die Universalität des Heils", in *Schriften* 12:251–85.

[8] *Christ sein* (Munich, 1977).

[9] "Jésus de Nazareth: Le récit d'un vivant", *Lumière et Vie* 134 (1977).

[10] *La Rédemption, mystère d'alliance* (Paris, 1964).

of man, a response that can bear the name of sacrifice, accepted by God, but is itself commanded and ordained by the God who accepts it. "The divine acceptance of the sacrifice is thus in the end only the continuation of God's action that was unfolded in the sacrifice itself."[11]

With this other phrase, too, we find ourselves again very close to Rahner's conception: "The death (of Christ) regarded as an event not passively suffered but freely consented to consists of an act of supreme disposition of self."[12]

Of course there are other emphases with Father Galot; he can speak of a debt to be paid, of a satisfaction required of Christ by God, and even of a reparation due to the divine love that has been wronged, but he rejects with horror any notion of vindictive justice: Christ was not punished —as the Protestants Luther, Calvin, and Karl Barth say— and consequently there is no divine wrath that would be appeased by the sacrifice of the Cross. The wrath of God is carried out, according to Galot, whether before the redemption (Romans 1, for example) or after it, only toward the men who do not want to accept the grace offered.[13]

---

[11] Ibid., p. 218.
[12] Ibid., p. 238.
[13] Ibid., pp. 104ff.

AN ATTEMPT TO FOCUS

Let us leave the theories now and try to take our bearings.

God's judgment

It seems naïve and superficial to me to wish simply to suppress everything that is said about God's *judgment* in the Bible, in the New Testament as well as in the Old. I am speaking here, not of what is said there about God's *justice*, which is a technical term for the clemency of the God of the Old Covenant, but about what concerns the inexorable judgment of God about all that is not conformed to holiness and to divine love.

In brief, we cannot make a distinction in God between apparently opposite attributes that are not in harmony in him. Whether Father Galot likes it or not, the wrath of God and his love, in the final analysis, are but one. Consult Saint Thérèse of Lisieux on that point, and she will confirm it for you.

"It is a fearful thing to fall into the hands of the living God", when "the Lord will judge his people", cries the author of the Letter to the Hebrews (10:31, 30)—a fearful thing for those who do not want to belong to him, because for the others, is there anything finer than to fall into the hands of the living God? "Our God is a consuming fire" the same letter says (12:29): it is the same burning essence that annihilates what is impure and glorifies what is conformed to it. This beautiful passage from the First Letter to the Corinthians (3:12ff.) confirms this for us: "The fire will test what sort of work each one has done. . . . If any man's work is burned up, he will suffer loss, though he himself will be saved, but only as through fire. . . .": "gold . . . is tested by fire" (1 Pet 1:7).

The event of the Cross

Now the Cross of Christ is judgment: "Now is the judgment of this world" (Jn 12:31; cf. 16:10-11). This inexorable judgment falls on the anti-divine reality of the world, on sin, but it is Christ who, according to Paul, "was made sin": here we meet again the great Pauline and Johannine texts quoted at the beginning.

Of course, it is not a question of the punishment of an innocent in place of the guilty; that notion does not appear anywhere. And it is not the concept of sacrifice that is introduced in the first place when we want to try to understand; its New Testament use is explained by its importance in the Old Testament, but the Letter to the Hebrews warns us that the whole sacrificial order *secundum ordinem Aaron et Levi* (according to the order of Aaron and Levi) is transcended in Christ and in his filial obedience. It is much rather the idea of substitution (I am dropping the adjective "penal") that is at the center, the apostolic *pro nobis*, with all that it contains of the mysterious.

In what direction can we turn in order to clarify this? In the direction, I think, of a voluntary and loving concentration in Jesus of all that in his brothers is opposed to God. I venture to suggest here, without having the time to develop it, that without this taking on of our sin, the complementary mystery of the Eucharist, by which, in an *admirabile commer-*

cium, Christ gives us what is his, would not be comprehensible.

— The experience of abandonment by God is undoubtedly situated at the center of the event of the Cross. This experience is that of sin given over to the hands of divine justice, to the fire of God's holiness. What is contrary to the latter can only be rejected by it. So that Christ might know this repulsion, he had, in some way, to identify himself with the sin of others. Saint Thomas assures us of it in the proper terms: the — cause of Christ's interior suffering was "the sins of mankind, for which he atoned": "Unde ea quasi sibi adscribit, dicens in Psalmo (21:2) 'Verba delictorum meorum'" ("Hence he ascribes them to himself, saying [Ps 21:2]: 'The words of my sins'") (*S. Th.* III, 46, 6).

Christ no longer wishes to distinguish between himself, the innocent, and his guilty brothers. He does not even want God to distinguish. Note that *adscribit* (ascribes) is an active verb. We must, as the preaching of the Gospel already does, suppose in the passive Passion, willed and enjoined by God, a sovereign spontaneity in Jesus, who, at the head of all those who will follow him, takes up his Cross (Lk 8:23; 14:27), — that Cross whose weight is out of proportion to his human strength alone. It will crush him, and more spiritually than physically.

A trinitarian mystery

How shall we conclude? And what, in the end, should be said of the so-called classic theory of Saint Anselm?

We can avoid the medieval side of his theory, that is, the reparation of God's injured honor, but we must substitute for it the idea of a divine love scorned by sin. Here, says Father Galot, "the testimony of Scripture is definite. Sin appears in it as an offense done to God."[14] For, as Father Guillet says, "God enters into the world and makes himself vulnerable."[15]

It would be absolutely unworthy of God to reveal first of all a justice that is at once gracious and demanding (*sedeq, mispat*) and then set aside all demands and all judgment in order to manifest only a love unconcerned about the behavior of men.[16] On that subject, Anselm cannot be matched.

The ever-recurring question remains: Is not this God who sends his Son into this dreadful death cruel, inhuman? For, it is dreadful in fact, for whoever thinks theologically, and it is not a question of sneering with a naïve cynicism, as this poor Dominican does:

> Jesus of Nazareth . . . suffered only a little. . . . [He] spent less than twenty-four hours in a police station, where he was beaten up between transfers from one local judge or administrator to another. He also experienced in his transfer to the place of execution the mixture of blows, insults, and mocking with which the clients of all police forces in the world are familiar. . . . It was even necessary to shorten the length of the torture so that everything would be finished before the great local religious feast. . . . In fact, he was very lucky. . . . It is not very respectful of the Lord to think that he would claim to have suffered more than you . . . on the pretext that he was God. Now that is absurd.[17]

[14] Ibid., p. 225.

[15] *Thèmes bibliques* (Paris, 1951), p. 99.

[16] Compare, for example, Romans 11:22: "Note then the kindness and the severity of God: severity toward those who have fallen, but God's kindness to you, provided you continue in his kindness, otherwise you too will be cut off."

[17] Jacques Pohier, *Quand je dis Dieu* (Paris, 1977), pp. 176–79.

There we have Christians, religious, joining the crowd who blasphemed at the foot of the Cross: "He saved others; let him save himself, if he is the Son of God" (see Mt 27:42–43; Lk 23:35).

If he is the Son of God, as the centurion affirms (Mt 27:54), then everything changes. Then we enter into a divine drama, a trinitarian drama, and as Christians we can no longer start from an Arian vision of the Divinity: a supreme God, named Father, giving orders to a subordinate or demi-God or superman who is going to carry them out, to say nothing of the Holy Spirit, who in this case could not be the common spirit of the Father and the Son, but at the most an authority subordinated to the Son.

As Christians, our point of departure can only be a *homoousios* Trinity, in which the liberty, dignity, and spontaneity of the Son and the Spirit are as divine as those of the Father, where the Son and the Spirit do not merely approve and carry out the orders of the creative and salvific plan of the Father but conceive that plan in the beginning in the most perfect unity with him.

And since it is the Son who, in this plan of salvation, will have to suffer in order to justify the fact that this world —even though blameworthy—might in the end be judged "very good", since it is he who will have to bear the weight of it like a spiritual Atlas, it is not enough to suppose that he acquiesces to the proposition of the Father; rather it must be admitted that the proposition proceeds originally from him, that he offers himself to the Father in order to sustain and save the work of creation. And it seems to me that this proposition of the Son touches the heart of the Father— humanly speaking—more profoundly even than the sin of the world will be able to affect it, that it works in God a wound of love already from the beginning of creation—if not to say that it is the sign and expression of this ever-open wound in the heart of the trinitarian life, a wound identical to the procession and circumincession of the Divine Persons in their perfect beatitude.

This wound is earlier than that which Saint Anselm had in mind, to wit, the offense made to the Father by sin and expiated by the Son, who was alone capable of this work that had to be supererogatory. And if the wound of which we are speaking was earlier than that, nothing prevents one from admitting that for the salvation of the world the Father sends the Son, guided on earth by the Spirit, who indicates to him, at every instant, the will of the Father and that this will might be both infinite love of creatures and infinite respect for the offer of the Son, which the Father has accepted and which the Spirit allows to be carried out up to supreme diastasis of the Father and the Son on the Cross, which is in truth the ultimate revelation of the tri-personality of God.

I do not think that this interpretation, which Moltmann and I have proposed at almost the same time, is gnostic or otherwise rash; rather I think that it alone succeeds in interpreting the Gospel facts without altering the weight of them: "ut non evacuatur crux Christi" (lest the cross of Christ be emptied of its power: 1 Cor 1:17).

4

Proclamation of the Mystery Today

How is this mystery to be proclaimed?

I do not see that it was any less scandalous in the first Christian century than in our own. It is just as incomprehensible for man as the existence of physical and moral evil.

Schillebeeckx and Küng affirm for us that the Cross of Christ did not in any way diminish the immense scandal of evil. Nevertheless, I think that the proclamation of the Cross can help men accept sufferings that often seem intolerable, to accept them, not because a God suffers in solidarity with them—how would that relieve them?—but because a divine suffering encompasses all these sufferings in order to transform them into prayer, into a dialogue in the midst of abandonment, thereby conferring on all human tragedies a meaning they would not have in themselves, a meaning that is in the end redemptive for the salvation of the world; all suffering being taken up secretly, mysteriously, into the sacrifice of the crucified Christ: of the Head who is inseparable from his members.

In our brief account, we have scarcely mentioned the link between the Cross and the Resurrection: we have presupposed it as obvious for all Christian thought. Without Easter, Good Friday would have no meaning. Without Easter, there would be no hope that suffering and abandonment might be tolerable. But with Easter, a way out becomes visible for human sorrows, an absolute future: more than a hope, a divine expectation.

REPLIES TO QUESTIONS

QUESTION: *Having limited his inquiry to four aspects of the re-demption in Saint Thomas, it seems to me that the speaker has not touched on one essential aspect: the restoration, or, better, the filial adoption that divinization is. Redemption is not only heal-ing*, redintegration ad integra, *but also access by the creature to the trinitarian communion*, entheiôsis. *Or is this an extension of substitution?*

FATHER VON BALTHASAR: "Redemption is not only healing; it is also access by the creature to the trinitarian life." This is true, but we already have access to the trinitarian life before faith. This is the whole intention of God, who wills the *théôsis*, the entrance into the trinitarian life. Redemption is a reopening. If you wish, it is truly the center of the event of our divinization, as I have tried to say by relating the Eucharist to the Cross. I believe it is necessary to do more. Christ truly gives himself to us, and he gives us what is his, because he has taken what is ours—sin—upon himself.

By seeing the two aspects at the same time, you have the answer to your question. But there is obviously, before faith, a grace that is already given, even to Adam.

QUESTION: *Is there not actually a certain opposition between say-ing of the Father that he is the initiator and source of the immense charity of Jesus for us and saying of Jesus that he preferred death to renouncing his reason for living?*

FATHER VON BALTHASAR: The Father, it is true, is the initia-tor and source of the immense charity of Jesus for us. But Jesus' reason for living is precisely to proclaim the charity of God, his very charity as Son of God. There is thus no opposition: it is the divine charity that is proposed by Jesus.

If you read Saint John, you will see how many times Jesus asks for love for himself; we will have to settle for one . . . "If you love me . . ." or "If you loved me", he says. There are perhaps eight or nine passages like that, I believe. That is his reason for living.

QUESTION: *How are we to understand that the intention of the Father and the Son is one in its conception or that the Son proposes it to the Father or that the decision originally proceeded from the Son?*

FATHER VON BALTHASAR: I am not saying that "the decision originally proceeded from the Son." I would say rather that this resolution of the Son has a character as original as that of the Father and the Spirit. There is not only one decision of the Father: that would be Arianism; but it is a trinitarian decree, in which the decision of the Son is as original as that of the Father. Obviously, that means that the Son is sent, since, according to Saint Thomas, the mission is the continuation of the procession. But that does not mean that the mission is secondary with respect to the plan formed by the Father.

In other words, "originally" must be understood in the tri-nitarian sense.

QUESTION: *Are you of the opinion that the theme of original sin must be integrated into catechesis, even for beginners, because of its link with Christ's redemption?*

FATHER VON BALTHASAR: I think that it is possible to appeal to the common and social sin of mankind without making long distinctions for beginners between original sin and the actual sin of the entire world. People understand rather quickly that there is a truly social and communal dimension in sin.

QUESTION: *What should be thought of the current expression among some consecrated souls: it is necessary to buy the souls of sinners, pay the price . . . ?*

FATHER VON BALTHASAR: There are, of course, consecrated souls who truly give themselves to the mystery of redemption. . . . Certainly it is not possible to enter into this mystery without being called to it in a special way. But in a general way, it is certain that all Christians are called to it. I am thinking of a spiritual book I have just reread, in which Christ demanded this special consecration of a large number of persons. But it is an act that must be distinguished from our gift of self in baptism, in our life as Christians.

II

Hans Urs von Balthasar

Mary and the Church in the Redemption

THE PARTICIPATION OF MARY
IN THE SACRIFICE OF CHRIST

I would like to present the subject to you from an unusual side. We have, or had, the custom of speaking of the "sacrifice of the Mass" (and many sacrificial expressions are still in the new Missal); we speak in this way because of the internal relationship between the Mass and the sacrifice of the Cross.

In our first part, we conceded that the sacrificial terminology was, like all the others, deficient, that is to say, inadequate; yet it remains obvious that the New Testament presents the mystery of the redemption to us as a supereminent fulfillment of all the forms of Old Testament sacrifices: bloody or unbloody, material or spiritual (the sacrifice of the lips, the broken heart, and so on).

When I speak of sacrifice, today as formerly, I call to mind above all a renunciation, whether of an object that is dear to me—that object can be a person to whom I am attached and of whom I must let go for some reason—or something of myself (I sacrifice my time to someone). And when we speak of the sacrifice of the Cross, we mean that Christ renounces his life for his brothers, for his sheep (according to Saint John), and, more profoundly, that he renounces the intimacy with his Father and, thereby, with himself, he who has his existence *eis ton kolpon toû patros*, turned toward the bosom of the Father (Jn 1:18). Now, the Father has disappeared, the eternal Word rises up in the void. —

If I now posed you the question: In the sacrifice of the Mass, what are you offering in the name of the Church, what are you renouncing? you would undoubtedly have some trouble finding an answer. You offer a little bread and wine: that costs you nothing, or very little; it is in no way comparable to the sacrifice of Solomon at the time of the dedication of the Temple: "twenty-two thousand oxen and a hundred and twenty thousand sheep" (1 Kings 8:63). You will respond to me: That offering was still not the true sacrifice; it is the Son himself whom we offer to the Father.

But what, then, is the meaning of this gesture? Within the context of the New Covenant, we can say that the Church offers to God the eternal incarnate Word as the only adequate response that the partner of the covenant can give him. Is that a sacrifice? In that offering, does the Church renounce something? Christ alone sacrifices himself. We can very well add that in sacrificing himself, he brings his Mystical Body into his sacrificial gesture, but that still demonstrates his action and not that of the Church.

I believe that the expression "sacrifice of the Mass" will remain obscure so long as we have not encountered that veiled woman at the foot of the Cross, who is the Mother of the Crucified and at the same time the icon of the Church. She is present at the self-gift of the Son, not able to intervene; but she is far from passive; a superhuman action is asked of her: consent to the sacrifice of this man who is the Son of God but also her own son. She would prefer a thousand times over to be tortured in his place. But this is not what is demanded of her; she has only to consent to it. Actively, she must let herself be stripped. She must repeat her initial Yes up to the end, but this end was virtually included in the first impulse.

This acquiescence of the Mother is the original form, reserved for the pure creature, of participation in the sacrifice of Christ. To have a sacrificial character, that is, of renun- — ciation in the gift to God, it is very clear that such an ac- quiescence can be realized only in pure love. The Mother is here the prototype of that Church which Paul describes as immaculate: "Ecclesia sancta et immaculata" (Eph 5:27), for which the consent to the Passion of Christ is infinitely painful but expressly required, for the solidarity that Christ wants to establish between himself and his Church is not content with a faith granted post factum, but demands a si- multaneous, instantaneous consent so that his sacrifice might be truly total: inseparably that of the Head and the members.

I would like to insert here a reflection that is not my own but Adrienne von Speyr's, in her dictations on the Gospel of John. According to her, the gesture of Mary of Bethany, who anoints the feet of Jesus with a very costly perfume of true nard, is also an ecclesial gesture of pure love, a gesture that the Lord accepts and which he interprets as an anoint- ing for his Passion and his burial. Mary the contemplative— "*personam Ecclesiae gerens*", as the Fathers say—would thus be the one who, in her total abandonment, acquiesces to the loss of what she loves more than anything.

Mary Magdalen, by contrast, the pardoned sinner, meets Jesus on Easter morning as he is in the process of rising, of going to his Father. Instinctively, she would like to cling to what she has sought in vain in the empty tomb; yet "Do not hold me, for I have not yet ascended to the Father; but go to my brethren . . ." (Jn 20:17); which means: Let me rise from the dead; consent to my disappearing, and turn —*personam Ecclesiae gerens*—toward my brothers in order to find me in them.

The mystery of the three Marys would thus consist, ac- cording to Adrienne von Speyr, in giving ecclesial consent to the fundamental articulations of the Christ event: Incarnation, Passion, Resurrection. Christ in his Incarnation did not wish at any moment to act alone, without the accompaniment of his Church. An isolated man has never existed; he is unthinkable: "It is not good", said God of this unhappy Adam in the midst of Paradise, "that the man should be alone" (Gen 2:18).

The disciples, representatives of the hierarchical Church, have not yet attained that pure love which acquiesces to all that Jesus does. It is true "You have loved me" (Jn 16:27), but "if you loved me" truly, "you would have rejoiced, because I go to the Father" (Jn 14:28). There is a discrepancy there: to Peter, who thinks he is able to follow but who is going to deny, it is said: "Where I am going you cannot follow me now; but you shall follow afterward" (Jn 13:36). It is after the Resurrection and after his denial that Peter will have to confess his greater love and that the promise of his death on a cross will be given to him along with the shepherd staff (Jn 21:15–19).

This discrepancy does not exist and cannot exist between the Mother and the Son. For the full consent of the Mother was already required at the time of the Incarnation of the Son. We do not need to begin again the long reflection of the Church on the implications of this request in order to arrive at the dogmatic conclusion: This Yes of Mary had to be a consent of total faith, without limit, without any restriction. For at least three reasons:

— Because God, in becoming incarnate in the Virgin, does not violate his creature.

— — Next, because this Mother had to be capable of introducing her Son into the fullness of Israel's religion, into perfect Abrahamic faith.

— Finally, because the Incarnation of the Word of God requires precisely a flesh that itself welcomes him faithfully; in other words, because the faith of this Mother had to encompass her whole person, body and soul, it had to be an incarnate faith.

MARY, MOTHER AND ARCHETYPE
OF THE CHURCH-BRIDE

Let us pause a moment at the first two reasons alleged: that of an active Yes required by God and that of the necessity of a mother capable of introducing her child into the religion of his ancestors.

With modern physiology and psychology, the philosophy of the woman has undergone incisive changes. On the one hand, we have known for at least a century that, in the act of generation, the woman is as active as the man, which runs contrary to what the Greeks and Scholastics supposed. It is undeniable, however, that the woman is the one who receives and that it is the man who gives. Conclusion: to — receive, to consent, to accept, to let things be is perhaps a no less active and creative attitude than that of giving, forming, imposing. And if in the Incarnation the part of man is taken by God, who is essentially the one who gives, indeed, who imposes, the part of the woman, who, as creature, accepts the divine gift, is far from being passive. Let us say, rather, that this acquiescence is the highest and most fruitful of human activities; in Pauline terms: faith is more fundamentally required than any works.

The idea that we have of the awakening of a child to the awareness of self has changed also. This awakening is accomplished only by the prompting of a person who, through his care, his love, his smile, demonstrates to the child that there is a world outside of him that can be trusted; and it is this risk of going out of oneself that engenders the awareness of self. Jesus, like any authentically human child, needed that call from a mother in order to acquire his human identity; he needed a whole education coming from outside in order to be assured within himself of the depths of his consciousness and of his mission as Son of the Father.

We can no longer agree with the opinion of Saint Thomas saying that Jesus could, in his acquired human knowledge, be taught by things whose ontological truth is unchanging but not by persons, who can subjectively err: "And since he is constituted Head of the Church, indeed, of all mankind, it was necessary that all receive through him not only grace but also the doctrine of truth—et ideo non fuit conveniens eius dignitati ut a quocumque hominum doceretur (and thus it did not befit his dignity that he should be taught by any man)" (*S. Th*. III, 12, 3).

For Saint Thomas, the Immaculate Conception was not yet in view, the grace of which, as we know, followed from the redemption by Christ and which witnesses to a circular movement between the Cross and the Incarnation, between Christ and Mary, between the new Adam and the new Eve. The trinitarian God alone is superior to this cyclical movement, but by becoming incarnate, the Son penetrates it, he conditions his own conditioning. For every child is conditioned by his mother.

Saint Paul alludes to this circle in speaking of the relation between the sexes: "In the Lord woman is not independent of man nor man of woman; for as woman was made from man, so man is now born of woman. And all things are from God" (1 Cor 11:11–12).

Things become complicated, however, when Paul applies the account of the creation of Eve from the side of Adam to Christ, the second Adam, who by his Passion presents to himself his holy and immaculate Bride, the Church (Eph 5:27). On the one hand, we learn from this that the ecclesial grace of Mary, like all grace, ensues from the Cross, but, on the other hand, since the grace of Mary the Mother is special, archetypal, we perceive a mysterious identity between the Church in her most profound authenticity and Mary. This identity was glimpsed as far back as Saint Irenaeus; it would be more and more clearly developed throughout the patristic age and into the early Middle Ages, whose symbolic iconography is well known: the woman standing beneath the Cross and collecting the blood of the Crucified in her chalice is Mary-Church without distinction.

I will not dwell on the details of the history of the relationship between Mary and the Church. Everyone knows the principal events of it.

Nor would I like to describe the abuses to which this mysterious identity has given rise; they could have been avoided if attention had been given to the fact that Christ is Son of the Father and Lord and Master, while Mary is pure creature and servant of God and that the Church, even insofar as Body and Bride of Christ, has never had, nor will ever have, any idea of adoring herself. Between Adam and Eve, the dignity of person is equal, even if we keep the legend of the woman formed from the side of the man. Between Christ and the new Eve—whether she be Mary or the Church—there is no parity: Mary is nothing but a servant, although full of grace; the Church is nothing but the receptacle of the fullness of Christ, and the vessel that collects is itself part of this fullness.

We would like, however, to try one step farther toward the interior of this mystery. According to Paul, the marital relationship between man and woman is sacred when it is contemplated in the light of the primordial couple: Christ and the Church. This relationship places us beyond sexuality, for the latter is inseparable from death; it produces innumerable individuals, all of the same kind, ephemeral, doomed from their birth to disappear. Christ crucified but risen came to conquer death. The last Adam, "Christ being raised from the dead will never die again; death no longer has dominion over him" (Rom 6:9). It is the same with his Bride, who is also his Body: in Mary, the Bride has already attained her full salvation; the latter as a whole will attain it one day in order to celebrate the eschatological wedding of the Lamb, as the Apocalypse describes it to us.

The archetypal relationship between the man and the woman goes beyond sexuality. Nevertheless, their relationship is fruitful: that is the meaning and the goal of the difference between them. The Apocalypse, and after it the Fathers, speaks to us of the fruitfulness of the Woman clothed with the sun: she gives birth not only to the Messiah but also to other children, "those who . . . bear testimony to Jesus" (Rev 12:17), which is to say, the faithful. Now in this relationship of fruitfulness, the role of the woman toward the man is always twofold: for him, she is mother and she is spouse. But if, on the level of the archetypal couple, she is essentially one, she must be both at once; or rather, temporal history intervening, she must as mother become spouse.

Mary begins by being the Mother, but at the Cross she ends by becoming the Bride, the quintessence of the Church. The Crucified says to his Mother: "Woman, behold your son" (Jn 19:27). Let us not forget that everything happens on a strictly suprasexual plane. On the sexual level, if the mother became spouse, we would be confronted with the drama of Oedipus, who, in order to marry his mother, had —without knowing it—to kill his father. In the Christian event, there is no place for the murder of the father, of

Joseph, for example, because there cannot be a human father. For in this whole perspective, it is clear that Mary can
become Bride or Church only if there was a virginal conception.

And, in order to draw some simple consequences, it is
also clear that, in the Church, virginity and celibacy, which
are in practical terms the same thing, have a special place. In
an absolutely privileged way, they give access to the fruitfulness of the archetypal couple. Now in Christianity, it is
fruitfulness that counts and not success. We can make our
own the adage of Martin Buber: "Success is not one of the
names of God." But the idea of fruitfulness is fundamental
in the New Testament: in the parables relating to growth, in
that of the fig tree, in that of the vineyard and vine shoots.

3

MARY CRUCIFIED IN FAITH
AND SELF-EFFACEMENT

— This fruitfulness that God expects of us and of his whole
Church is founded on the divinity of the Bridegroom who
communicates his own fruitfulness to the human Bride. In
order for Mary to be capable of acceding to the Cross, an
ever more profound, merciless initiation is necessary for
her, applied without regard for her by her Son. From the
beginning, she provides the perfect faith of Abraham, docil-
ity without reserve. But this faith is not in her, as in the
prophets, to become hardened against all the adversities—
"I make of you this day a fortified city, an iron pillar, and
bronze walls" (Jer 1:18)—she is submit to all the humiliations, to feel them, to accept them like the sword that is to
pierce her heart.

Consequently, all the Gospel scenes where the Son encounters his Mother will be scenes of humiliation:

— at the Temple, Mary does not understand why the Son
has done that to her;

— at Cana, she is dismissed: "Woman, what have you to
do with me?" (Jn 2:4);

— at the time of her visit, she is not even received, and the
Son designates his listeners as his brothers and his mother;

— when the woman in the crowd blesses "the breasts that
you sucked", Jesus again turns the attention away from his

Mother: "Blessed rather are those who hear the word of God and keep it" (Lk 11:27–28).

After all these rejections and all the anxieties and incomprehension of Mary, she will be ready to hear, beneath the Cross, the last word of the Son, the hardest perhaps, for he withdraws from her his sonship in order to substitute another for it: "Woman, behold your son" (Jn 19:26). And it is precisely in this way that the perfect union between the two is accomplished: just as the Father abandons his Son, the Son separates himself from his Mother. This form of union was necessary so that Mary—who henceforth would have to form the center of the Church—might know from experience the mystery of the redemption and might be able to transmit it to her new children.

The specifically Christian humility is learned in no other way than by formal and repeated humiliations. Just as Christ is humiliated all the way to the Cross in order to be able to fulfill the mission of the Father, so he humiliates his Mother and bestows on her her ecclesial mission through a final humiliation. He will proceed in the same way with Peter, who, at the moment when his treason is recalled, will be invested with his responsibility as shepherd.

For Mary, her new mission includes a particularly humiliating aspect: in becoming the mother of a disciple—even if the latter is the beloved disciple of Jesus—she enters into an intimate relationship with the ecclesiastical hierarchy. Throughout all the first chapters of Acts, we see in fact that Peter and John are inseparable; and we witness an ultimate dispossession of Mary by seeing her disappear, in Luke, into the assembled crowd imploring the descent of the Spirit.

Such is the result of Mary's education by Christ, which

transforms the faith of Israel in her (which is, of course, perfect) into an ecclesial and crucified faith. Into a faith that, in a certain sense, collaborates with the redemption and could well be called a co-redemptive faith if that word were not too open to misunderstandings.

For, from beginning to end, Marian faith is acquiescence and not personal initiative. She lets things be and allows them to be done without doing them herself. She does not invent means for humiliating herself but does not refuse any measure taken by her Son in order to conform her more to himself. The Yes of the servant remains the inner form of all following steps, however unexpected and shocking they might be. That imperturbable Yes, offered through all the nights and incomprehension, is the foundation of what can be called collaboration, Marian and ecclesial co-redemption.

For henceforth it is no longer necessary to separate Mary and the Church. Certainly the collaboration of Mary is of a unique quality because of her preservation from any original sin. But she herself does not insist upon her personal privileges; she lives in union with all the brothers and sisters of Christ. And why would we refuse to believe that grace can purify a great number of souls and render them, too, capable of collaborating in the redemptive work of the Son? Saint Paul, with great boldness, designates himself and others as "collaborators" (*synergoi*) with God, with the Truth, with the Kingdom of God. He has in mind a principally external, missionary work, but one that implies—at least with him, but also with others—an interior dedication that, without his knowledge, secretly bears Marian marks: extreme humiliations that push him back to the *last place* and, on the other hand, fruitfulness that is feminine because it is ecclesial, which painfully gives birth to the communities.

With all that it is not our intention to encourage a certain dolorism, more morbid than Christian, that would seek to sink into the sufferings of the Crucified. If Christ, in Luke, commands us to carry our cross every day, he implies very precisely that this dull, ordinary cross consists in persevering at every moment in the Marian Yes, which transforms everyday mishaps as much as possible into situations that are fruitful in Christian terms.

It is always Christ who gives a share in his Cross, but the form of this participation always remains ecclesial and, thus, Marian, in priests and religious no less than in the ordinary faithful. But if Saint Paul affirms that he finds his joy "in my sufferings for your sake" and that "in my flesh I complete what is lacking in Christ's afflictions for the sake of his body, that is, the Church" (Col 1:24), he is very conscious of enduring these sufferings in favor of the Church as a grace that the crucified Lord grants him. "Was Paul crucified for you?" (1 Cor 1:13).

Nevertheless, in a certain sense, the circular course we have noted between the Mother and the Son continues, although in another manner, between Christ and his Church.

Christ takes up the *hysterēmata tōn thlipseōn toū Christoū*, the elements lacking to the Cross of Christ and that are provided him by the compassionate Church, in his original Cross in order to make a whole indivisible offering of them to God the Father as a unique act of love that exceeds the weight of sin. But everything the ecclesial body adds is derived from the Cross; it is through grace from the Head that the Body can collaborate; it is an effect of the fullness of Christ that a place is reserved for us in the redemptive work.

This observation can help us understand better the primordial reciprocity between Mary and her Son. If it is true that the grace of Mary's preredemption derives from the

Cross and that Mary has, in a certain sense, collaborated in the Cross through her Yes, it is nevertheless absolutely impossible for Mary to have collaborated in her own redemption. The Marian and ecclesial Yes is always response, consent, never the first action. The latter, in the domain of grace, belongs to God alone. Even the faith of Abraham was only a response to the divine call, and the response itself was a grace granted together with the call. Likewise, the Yes of Mary, even if it was prior to the Incarnation, was a response subsequent to a divine word, which in itself contained the entire redemption plan, including the Cross, and all that it encompassed.

No one who gives witness to his faith, his respect, his veneration to Christ would be able to refuse a similar respect and veneration to his Mother. Not adoration, but respect and veneration, love and gratitude. We will refrain from any exaggeration that confuses the divine and the human. But we will no less refrain from separating what God has united, the Christ-Head and his Body the Church along with, in her, this privileged member who is Mary, the Mother of the Head.

4

Mary, Model for the Church

We said above that the Church has never had any idea of venerating herself, indeed, of adoring herself. But it is appropriate to add now: each of us who are members of the Church has had access to an infinitely mysterious reality that is prior to us and that will always transcend us: the union of Christ and his Church.

It is to this union that we owe ourselves; through it, we are what we are: Christians; we live, we work and suffer for it. As Catholics, we cannot maintain a relation of personal piety with God and with his Christ if we isolate that from Mary-Church.

At the center of the Church is Christ. For a Christian, it is impossible to see in the Church a purely sociological reality that one could judge and criticize solely from the point of view of the human sciences. There might be justifiable criticism of her conformity with the attitude of Christ, but — one must be careful, as we have said, about measuring this conformity according to categories of success rather than of fruitfulness.

Let us not forget that Jesus came to free men from their slavery to sin, that he declined every offer of a secular messianism, that he failed in his attempt to convert Israel, and that it was only *the hour*—the hour of God and of darkness— that decided the victory. We who are trying to follow him, we will work with all our power to promote the Kingdom of God, justice between men, but first of all by changing the dispositions of hearts, by opening them to those of the Heart of Jesus, for the Church we represent has authentic life only — in being conformed to the sentiments of that Heart. All the fine sociological programs promulgated and made public by the ecclesiastical authorities or by the offices and committees they institute and encourage have Christian value only when subject to that criterion, and the ordinary member of the faithful is very well able to apply this criterion to them and to compare these *ukases* with the word of the Gospel.

It is certainly a significant fact that the French episcopacy often meets at Lourdes, a fact that can signify only one thing: that it is ready to conform the ecclesial sense of the hierarchy to the ecclesial sense of Mary herself, the purest expression of the *sentire cum ecclesia*, since she is the archetypal Church, modeled by Christ.

I will say nothing of the numerous—for many, too numerous—apparitions of the Virgin during recent decades; some may be of doubtful authenticity, and we know how delicate is the translation of a heavenly message into human words, how subject to caution are these messages that circulate among the faithful.

Yet it seems that at the present hour the archetypal heavenly Church is taking to heart the spiritual direction of the empirical earthly Church. It would be enough for the latter, moreover, to remember the fundamental attitude of Mary, to meditate on it, and to put it into practice in order to find the trail she must follow. It would not then be a matter of special devotions, which are useful for some but in no way obligatory for all. It would rather be a matter of a deep, general orientation that could be called Marian and that would be the central motive for the course of the Church: consent to the fundamental demands of the Gospel such as it presents itself, and not such as we transform it into a postchristian ideology.

Let us not forget, in the midst of everything, this humility of Mary—*respexit humilitatem ancillae*—that must be perfected by ever-renewed humiliations. The Church will do her redemptive work in these times only if she agrees to be humiliated and to experience her humiliations in a Christian spirit. It is not a matter only of enduring a setback and of compensating for the bitterness of it by starting up new utopian programs for the transformation of social bodies and for solidarity with the impoverished masses or the Third World. We are not permitted to cushion the shock of humiliations; rather, more courage is necessary in order to submit to the blows and the wounds and thus to transform them into a new potential for love.

5

THE REQUIREMENT OF
THE PRESENT TIME

I will end by returning to the beginning of our first meditation. It is men of the Church and spiritual people that
the young people of today greatly need and desire to en-
counter. If they do not find them among the priests and
religious, they will go to seek them among the yogis and
illumined. The latter abound in Europe and gather a good
harvest. Most of their followers are people disgusted, dis- —
couraged, disillusioned by the Church; by meaningless or
false religious services, sermons, and catecheses. They are
hungry and thirsty, and they are going away across the desert
in search of a spring. They are victims of conflicting and ir-
reconcilable ideologies: Buddhist and Marxist, vertical and
horizontal, without understanding that Christ alone reconciles in his Cross the two dimensions in which human existence extends: toward God and toward neighbor. —

Or then these young people have met men of the Church
who were not, or who did not appear to be, spiritual, and
through such encounters the gap between Christ and his
Church was widened for them. Christ, yes; Church, no.
— Sooner or later they will have to perceive that a Christ
without a Church remains a phantom, that he never existed
without his Mother and never preached without his disciples, to whom he transmitted his powers and handed over
his Body and his Blood, that we know nothing about him
except through the testimony of ecclesial faith. It is true, one

of the Twelve betrayed him, and betrayals have continued down through the history of the Church and increase today. It is for us to make the Church visible in her purest, truest essence: the Church of the saints, of the witnesses and the martyrs, the Church of those who are called the faithful and who are truly so. They are everywhere. Let us take care that they do not despair. We will have to render an account of them.

—The Church, the Body of Christ, is the universal sacrament of salvation. She is, in Christ, at once the sign and the means of intimate union with God and, thereby, of the unity of the whole of the human race. The last council said this repeatedly. That does not mean that she does not have to deal with the many serious questions that torment mankind and that cannot help but concern her, too: hunger, oppression, disarmament . . . But it does mean, above all, that she must, with Christ and through him, give to us his Body and his Blood, give of herself for the salvation of the world. Or —rather, since she is Bride, since Mary is her heart—she must consent to being given, allow herself to be distributed.

After having done what she is able to do—actively—she must still act over and beyond her ability, because God has the power to draw from her, in the Passion of Christ, energies that she does not suspect but to which, through grace, she can still consent. Read Madeleine Delbrêl or Adrienne von Speyr;[1] they will explain to you with more simplicity and urgency what I have wanted to say to you.

---

[1] Cf. below, part 3: "Flashes of the Passion", fragments of meditations by Adrienne von Speyr.

REPLIES TO QUESTIONS

QUESTION: *How should Paul VI's declaration "Mary, Mother of the Church" be understood?*

FATHER VON BALTHASAR: Naturally many titles can be given to Mary and to this mysterious circular course between her and the Church.

It is very obvious that this name should not be pushed too far. One obvious meaning can be given it, for example, in seeing something Marian in the Woman of the Apocalypse, who is the Mother of the Son and the Mother of the other children to whom she gives birth, who then represent the faithful, which means, fundamentally, the Church. In this sense, she is superior, she is first.

In another sense, which the Pope knows as well as we, she is within the Church, a member of the Church; as Saint Augustine said and as has been repeated: She is not outside the Church. These images with which you are familiar—neck or heart or other things—can be taken to show that she has a superiority.

But both are there at one and the same time. And I think that it is good and just to show this superiority as well by that immense mantle of the Virgin that encircles all Christians. She is truly the Mother of Christians and, thus, of the Church. I think that such an image is indispensable: it is necessary to us.

QUESTION: *Can it be said that Jesus is Savior because he is himself quasi-saved by God (cf. Phil 2: God spared him)? Salvation is thus for us a mystery of the solidarity of man with Jesus in his Passion.*

FATHER VON BALTHASAR: No, we cannot say that. Because, if we truly hold that he is the Son of God par excellence, he is not *saved* by God; rather he is *Savior*. From what would he be saved? Since he is the Word of God, the Word of the Father, and since, in the end, this Word became incarnate in our human nature, it is not possible to say that he is saved by God. "God spared him", you say, and "salvation is thus for us a mystery of the solidarity of man with Jesus in his Passion." I think I said that this aspect of solidarity is jus- tifiable, is necessary, but we cannot remain at the idea of solidarity. That would be of no benefit to us if there were not the true redemption of which we have spoken. And it cannot be said that "God spared him": I do not know where you have found this passage in Philippians 2 . . . God did not spare him. He restored him to life because Christ went to the limit of obedience to the Father, and the descent of Christ, in the hymn of Philippians, is identical to the ascent, as Saint John says. Which is to say that the glorification of the Son of man is at one and the same time the Cross and the Resurrection.

QUESTION: *Is not Mary, too, like the Church, Savior along with Jesus because she is saved by him?*

FATHER VON BALTHASAR: She is so, along with Jesus, in the sense in which I have tried to explain. But it is always neces- sary to be absolutely mindful of this difference between the one who does and the one who consents. If you insist abso- lutely on co-redemption, I have said that it was possible pro- vided you succeeded in showing, in this term, the analogy between what Christ does and what Mary does. But there is an immense difference. You must have both together. If you say simply "co-redemptrix", everyone will see in that a kind of univocity.

QUESTION: *What role does Mary now play in the Church and in the life of every Christian?*

FATHER VON BALTHASAR: Perhaps that could be deduced from what I said at the end: that it is a matter truly, primarily, and essentially of consent, and not of inventing what might be done; it is a matter of consenting to what the Holy Spirit wants to do through us, like the way in which the Spirit wants to bring the word of the Gospel to life today.

This consent to what is asked of us: that, I believe, is the essence. And often our own inventions, which stem from certain external, sociological givens, and so on, prevent us from listening to the word of the Spirit.

I leave room for all the particular and quite central ecclesial, Marian devotions that you might have, each and every one of them.

FATHER BORIS BOBRINSKOY: It seems to me that our Orthodox contribution might be to show how, in the mystery of Christ as well as in that of his Mother and in that of the Church, just as in her total maternity as spouse and also in that of her children, of her faithful, it is in this birth and growth in the Holy Spirit that Mary is what she is.

For example, the reaction of the Orthodox is rather negative with regard to the formulas that express the dogma of the Immaculate Conception. It seems to me that basically we would have preferred to see that formulated in a positive manner, not as a right or as a prerogative, but as a fullness, the fullness of life in the Holy Spirit, a fullness of which Mary was the keeper, through grace, through the eternal thought of God, since the beginning, and in which she grew until the moment of her entrance to the Temple. The whole hesychast tradition, and the Palamite in particular, shows how the Mother of God lived this interior process of maturing, ripening, this ceaseless meditation on the name of God, then, from the Annunciation, on the name of Jesus.

This is why what Father von Balthasar has recalled about the successive humiliations of Mary is very valuable. But I will say, in order to situate us in the climate of the Johannine Gospel, that the humiliation and the glory are but one. And, consequently, at the very moment of her strongest humiliations, Mary grew at the same time: it was given her to accede and to grow from fullness to fullness, from glory to glory.

To conclude, I will say that Mary's role seems to me to be assuredly archetypal, not only of that of the Church, but also, in the Holy Spirit, of each one of us. I believe that, in the Christian tradition of the East and of the West, it is shown how we can, in our turn, realize within ourselves this mystery of Mary, of virginal conception, through a rediscovered virginity of which the Fathers speak: a virginal conception, birth, growth, blossoming of Jesus in us and of us in him.

I believe, thus, that there is in this an analogy, but one that can be explained only by the Holy Spirit. And in the Holy Spirit, all the terms are admissible, including that of co-redemptrix: the Orthodox Church does not mind praying to Mary by saying: "Holy Mother of God, save us!"— which, generally shocks many of our Protestant brothers.

FATHER VON BALTHASAR: I would not like to add anything to such beautiful words. I believe that we are truly, really, absolutely in agreement. This positive idea of Mary's sanctity, of the *panagya*, has, moreover, been declared first of all in the East and came later to the West. The East has always seen this fullness in Mary, which is better expressed positively than negatively.

Besides, as you all know, we have slightly different conceptions of original sin, and thus that cannot coincide absolutely on the level of concepts, if we keep the Western concepts of original sin—which are rather controversial today. If, then, we leave that aside, if we see the positive side, as you have set it forth, I believe that the visions coincide still more.

III

Adrienne von Speyr

FLASHES OF THE PASSION

There where the efficacy of all healing ceases, the unforeseeable and gratuitous fruitfulness of the Cross still subsists. And, as the following fragments show, we are all summoned, as a community as well as individually, from a distance or up close, in one manner or another, to be at the foot of this Cross.

HANS URS VON BALTHASAR

I

THE FIRE OF GOD IS A SUFFERING

The suffering on the Cross is the expression of the love within God. The expression chosen by God to show us the mystery of his love; in order to be able to reveal itself, love suffers.

There we also find a mystery of time and of beyond time. We are used to loving in time, with the resources of our nature, bound everywhere to time and to our objectives. When it is a question of God, we somehow adapt our temporal love to him. In faith we of course know that God is and has a love that is infinitely greater than us; yet, we try to reduce it at all costs to our own categories, to love him as it is given us: in half-heartedness and in time. When we meet with suffering, there is nothing more urgent for us to do than to console ourselves by saying that it will pass. We are surprised if that does not happen quickly; we are even more so if our suffering outlives love. Then we go and take measurements. We measure one time against another and the force of events: suffering or love. Now, when God comes into the world in order to suffer for us, he takes with him the measurements of eternity; he prepares for the Cross with the strength of eternal love and experiences as a man an immeasurable suffering that corresponds to his divinity and to his divine love. It is not the motive of the Cross, sin, that determines the measure of suffering but the divine will to redeem us in order to make us enter into his infinite love.

If God brought his love to earth as pure fire, perhaps he

would find a few men who would not yet be completely hardened by sin and would surrender to his fire. But his plan is to save us all. And he cannot do this by transmitting the fire of love from one man to another; he must transform his fire into suffering. But, because he himself is all purity and because nothing in him can be consumed, he takes within himself as fuel the sin of the world and burns it within himself, in the human nature that the Father has given him; he suffers through each of us.

This fire of suffering in which he experiences sin he can henceforth use both as fire and as love at the same time, everywhere there are men to be purified: in confession, in the Eucharist, and even where men can no longer act themselves: in purgatory. It is the fire that he came to cast on the earth; but between heaven and earth, it is transformed into suffering. It was given to him twice: he received it in order to cast it on the earth, and he took it back again from suffering and from death in order to accomplish his purifying work in all men. He is transformed or lets himself be transformed by the Father in order to lead to its conclusion the unique mission of the redemption through all its states: Incarnation, suffering, death, Resurrection, judgment. In these transformations, love becomes suffering: the Lord experiences first of all the fire on himself in order to be able then, through his fire of suffering, to lead men to love.

Excerpt from *Mystique objective*
(*Objektive Mystik*, in *Nachlassbände* 6:329–30)

2

"Let Us Go and Suffer with Him"

"My soul is very sorrowful, even to death." It is the soul of the human nature assumed by Jesus, the soul that he never ceases to open to his disciples but to which he never refers, all the same, except indirectly. They grasped what expressed his soul most decisively in his teaching, in his miracles, in his love for them and for all men. They could deduce from his actions and his behavior that his soul was fully human. But now, he reveals to them that his soul is filled with sorrow, that it overflows with it even to the point of touching death, so full that one drop more would take away his life. By expressing it and by not keeping that for himself, he invites the disciples to take part in his sorrow. He unveils it to them like a secret; he exposes it to their eyes so that they might be in communion with him in his own sense, in the sense of the New Covenant, in the sense of the Cross as a gift to the Father, and so that they might, insofar as possible, remain in the state that is his own. Before leaving them, he wants once more to give himself, perfecting the eucharistic gift. Of course, he withdraws into solitude in order to be alone with the Father, but not before having shown them his soul and asking them to remain and watch with him, to do the same thing as he, and, despite the few steps that separate them, to be united with him in the sorrow and anguish that fill his soul. That should be the Christian prayer of accompaniment. If he had renounced this request, if he had not opened his soul, the link that unites us to him in the Eucharist would have seemed limited in time and in its content. He would have handed himself over to them in a certain state, while keeping certain others for himself. On the contrary, the communion has invited them to participate in the whole of his states and to place their prayer in his in a way of which they had not had any idea until then. The one with the other and the one in the other: that is a property of the Church that overcomes distance, and not only distance in space or between persons, but also that of content: he is going to ask *something* in his prayer, and they, too, will ask *something*; but in the diversity of content, the acts touch each other and pass into each other.

"Watch with me." By asking them to watch with him, he gives them the possibility of attaining, against the background of their fatigue, so to speak, a certain form of affliction by which their prayer is—from a distance—made similar to his own. This request of the Lord clearly shows to the entire Church that Christian ascesis must accompany the Lord in his Passion.

> Excerpt from the *Passion selon
> saint Matthieu*, on Matthew 26:38
> (*Passion nach Matthäus*, pp. 45–47, with omissions)

3

Nailed to Sin

They crucified him. He received those holy wounds, which men consider marks of infamy, as an indelible sign by which each one can recognize that this body was treated like that of a criminal. He will want no longer to be separated from these marks; he will carry them into his eternity. We will always see in him that he was crucified. The nails are the sign of sin that penetrates him. They cause a suffering in him that is first of all the physical suffering corresponding to such a wound, but which infinitely surpasses it (since they are the nails of sin) and which, running right through him, lets nothing escape but seizes him entirely, nailing him to itself. It is by the sin of the world, which takes the concrete form of these nails, that he is fixed in place, immobilized, plunged into total passivity. At the moment when he is nailed to the Cross begins that phase of the Passion which no longer consists merely in bearing, enduring, letting it be done. Those who crucify him and who have already crucified others perceive the gift that he makes of himself and do not understand it.

> Excerpt from the *Passion selon saint Matthieu*, on Matthew 27:35

4

THE RESUMPTION OF ALL
SUFFERING IN THE CROSS

On the Cross the Lord does not show merely that he allows his grace to flow visibly over all, over all those who surround the Cross and also over all those who earlier, in the Old Covenant, possessed faith, accepted his promises as he gave them, and remained ready to live out the accomplishment of them—when he wished to grant that to them—but he also shows that he can make use of all they have accomplished for him. And thus that he does not suffer his Passion simply for sins, but that he is in a mysterious compassion with all believers. In a compassion that does not amount for him to any easing—because he suffers entirely for them, too, and completes their suffering by his own—but that is nevertheless not devoid of meaning for the redemption. He assumes all the trials of their faith, of their suffering, and of their availability and opens wide to them the grace that flows from the Cross. It is not only the sins of the entire world that rush to the Cross in order to be effaced; it is also all the beginnings of faith and suffering that go there to find their fulfillment. In the Cross is also found the Lord's acknowledgment of all the precursors of the New Covenant, an expression of gratitude that he manifests to them by carrying their sufferings to their culmination and thereby making of Job and the other great men of patience saints, as it were, of the New Covenant. He completes the Old Covenant in the New because, already in his Incarnation, he was taking up within himself the totality of the Old Covenant and fulfilling it through his divine grace.

Excerpt from "Le Sermon sur la montagne"
on Matthew 5:39 (*Bergpredigt*, p. 122)

5

THE ONE WHO SUFFERS
AND THE WITNESS

The Son perseveres in the "ever more" of availability since no upper limit is shown him of what he must go through. Just like the Spirit, he now accomplishes his mission *without measure*. It is for the Father to measure and to determine. The Son remains open in his suffering, and the Spirit, too, in introducing him into suffering.

The law of suffering demands, in a way, two partners: one suffers as he can; the other is there as witness, who disposes and serves as mediator. It is the role of the Spirit never to stop revealing anew the reason for suffering. The Son cannot arrange his suffering: undergo one suffering for this and another for that. Otherwise he would himself be in a position to measure. So it is up to the Spirit to present the things, not of course in such a way that they would seem determined, one after the other, by the suffering, but only by adding to it ever anew. Nothing here is comparable to human collaboration. And perhaps the Son and the Spirit are not truly to meet each other, either, in the Passion; they, so to speak, do not speak the same language, for if the Son still recognized the Spirit as the Spirit of the Father, he could not be abandoned. He would feel a relief; he would have hope. So he understands well the instructions of the Spirit, but he does not see any correspondence to them in his own suffering. There are as if two levels of truth: the one in the mind of the witness, the other in mind of the one who suffers. If these two levels coincide, the truth of the Father would be obvious for the Son; he would, insofar as God, hand over this man Jesus in one way or another to the suffering and would collaborate with the Spirit as spectator. But this would not be a human-divine suffering. So the Son cannot for the moment be on the level of the Spirit; he is on that of his mission in the world; the Father measures out for him the part of his divine consciousness that he needs for that according to the demands of the mission.

At the end, the dying Son places the Spirit back in the hands of the Father. The Spirit does not turn back with his own movement; he is sent back. It is the ultimate consent of the Son to the Cross that the Father has given him. It belongs to the mission of the Son and the Spirit for them to separate at the Cross. . . .

Insofar as the Son had the Spirit close to him as rule, he was obedient toward the Spirit. Now, it is the Spirit who obeys the Son by returning in the undivided obedience of the Father. The Son thus inaugurates the sending of the Spirit that he completed after Easter: sending first toward the Father, then toward the Church and the world.

Excerpt from *Mystique objective*
(*Objektive Mystik*, in *Nachlassbände* 6:410–11)

6

THE ONE WHO SUFFERS AND
THE WITNESS IN THE CHURCH

"But rejoice in so far as you share Christ's sufferings, that you may also rejoice and be glad when his glory is revealed" (1 Pet 4:13). If Christians are filled with the living knowledge of the Lord, they can have for him only feelings of joy and gratitude. Whatever he might offer to them, these feelings will not be changed, will not depend on their own appreciation of his gifts. Thus it is that they will rejoice even when he gives them suffering, provided that it be a true participation in the sufferings of the Lord. He can associate us with his Passion, make us participate most intimately with his suffering, and even every now and then make the limit that separates his suffering from ours be erased, so that, in this suffering we will truly suffer in his name, through him, in the power and love that unite him to the Father. We must not fear this and let ourselves take back, in the night of suffering, the joy underlying this being allowed to suffer with Christ. The joy may have been sent as a deposit; it may have become insensible; it must above all be there, even in the most profound suffering, as grateful joy that we know to be so profoundly anchored in the Lord that it does not disappear even when our whole capacity for feeling is required by the suffering.

Peter knows the beginning, the end, the determination of suffering, and he knows that all—beginning, end, and measure—remain inserted into the suffering of the Lord, at the place the Lord himself determines and that he arranges according to his needs and according to the measure to which we abandon ourselves to him. The Lord is the only one to have his own suffering at his disposal. The Church does not have a word to say in this sphere. The decision to allow someone to participate in his suffering is in the hands of the Lord alone; the Church can at the most guide the one who suffers, communicate to him a better understanding of his suffering. This is why Peter must speak of it, explain the meaning of suffering, awaken the availability for it, show, in the end, how the Church, too, makes use of its fruit. If the Church has here the right to speak, she must also possess an intimate understanding of those sufferings that make her indebted to the Lord and to those who suffer. There where the Lord awaits the fruit of a suffering, the Church must make every effort to see that he receives the full value; and where someone who suffers wants to give himself entirely, she must strive to make him produce the full value. And because believers are members of the Lord, the member who does not suffer (represented by the ministerial Church) must open to God the one who suffers and help him realize as fully as possible what is demanded. The one who suffers must be open, so that he has more space for suffering than the Lord wants to offer him. It would also be necessary to make the Lord closer to him so that he remains capable of acceding to the demand of Peter that we rejoice also in suffering. So that he might know that he must accomplish even the most difficult thing in the joy of the Lord, without, however, experiencing it at the time, and that the Church keeps this joy in reserve for him. The Church does not have the right, in the face of such suffering, to be content with the role of spectator. No one in the Church, moreover, would be only a spectator. Someone may have as a ministry the contemplation of the one who must suffer; but this mandate of contemplation is then only one part of his broader ministry, and the ministry is only what is demanded of him.

To rejoice when we suffer means to place, when we are suffering, our subjective suffering into the objective good news of the Lord, just as the Son hanging on the Cross suffers in a certain joy as a deposit made at being able to glorify the Father through his suffering. In returning to the Father, the Son will live there the perfect joy of the glorification of the Father, just as he can in his own joy glorify the Father, the joy that he will offer us *at the revelation of his glory.*

Excerpt from the *Lettres catholiques* on 1 Peter 4:13 (*Katholische Briefe* 1:380–82)

7

"JESUS SAYS: I THIRST"

The Lord is at the end of his strength, emptied of his sub-
stance. He can go no farther. The sin that he carries is infinitely heavy, even heavier that he had imagined. One can
almost say: heavier than the Father thought. As if it were
necessary to be man in order to feel the greatness of the sacrifice, and not only to be man, but to have the experience
of it here and now in order to know what it is. The entire
soul of the Son, to its innermost reaches, is employed in
bearing the sin, in such an affliction and distress that there
is no place for anything else. But the suffering of the soul
does not make him forget the bodily pain.

He does not suffer in certain parts of himself; he suffers totally in the whole of his being. Whence his appalling
thirst, which assails him as the ultimate torment, as what he
was not expecting because all the rest was already so heavy
and which comes now to be added as the burning mark of
the divine ever-more. It is not possible to distinguish in this
thirst what is spiritual from what is corporal. It seems at first
that the two dimensions separate into two halves: the soul
has so much to do with the sin of the world that it cannot
deal with the body; the body is so exhausted that it pays
no more attention to the soul. Then, there is this thirst, in
both the body and the soul at once, and it reunites more
closely than ever the two separated halves. The unity that
they form is that of total exhaustion, of the inability to bear
any more.

And then, it is as if this strange, unnatural, but also new and unexpected unity announced already the resurrection of the flesh, as if, within the spiritual suffering, the body were signaling to the soul, through this common thirst, that it is still there, that it is enduring the suffering with it, that it shares a body with it as much as it can. It can render to this overburdened soul the service of carrying its burden with it by taking upon itself the spiritual thirst and by showing itself capable, finished as it is, of taking on itself something of the infinite capacity of suffering of the human-divine soul of the Redeemer. When the soul rises to eternal life, it will want no longer to be separated from this part that is linked by the bond of thirst. And God will make it a gift of this body in eternal life: in memory of the creative act of the Father, of the Incarnation of the Son, but also in memory of their common suffering on the Cross, which weaves between the two bonds so close that a separation is henceforth unthinkable. So powerful is this thirst that the Lord relates it to the unity of his person: I thirst! That is the guarantee of the resurrection of the flesh.

Excerpt from the *Passion nach Matthaüs*
on John 19:28, pp. 176–77

Postscript

Jacques Servais, S.J. (2005)

I

THE THOMIST DOCTRINE
OF THE REDEMPTION

"If Christ suffered death," declares Saint Thomas, "it was voluntarily, so as to make satisfaction for us"; he was not at all as if compelled by the death sentence that struck the first parents according to the warning of Genesis 2:17, for he himself "was not obliged to die".[1] In the eyes of Aquinas, like the whole tradition he inherits, the death of Jesus does not have in the first place the meaning it possesses for ordinary men; it is not the simple, inevitable outcome of earthly destiny: it is a unique event whose specific value resides in the free gift of the God-made-flesh for the salvation of the world. In it is consummated the work of our deliverance and of our rebirth to eternal life.

The Angelic Doctor finds the decisive proof that, in the economy as it was fixed from all eternity, the redemption was to be accomplished through the Cross, in the affirmation of the Scriptures and in particular the passage reported by John 3:14-15, in which he reads, as do contemporary exegetes, an allusion to the elevation of the Cross: "And as Moses lifted up the serpent in the wilderness, so must the Son of man be lifted up, that whoever believes in him may have eternal life."

If, in accordance with the expression of the Gospel, the Passion was necessary, of what order is this necessity? For

[1] *S. Th.* III, 35, 6 ad 1.

Thomas, it can obviously not be a question of an absolute necessity, for neither the nature of God nor, he insists, the nature of man demands that Christ suffer. He emphasizes the absolute freedom of the author of our redemption. But would it not have been, in itself, completely appropriate for Christ, true God and true man, "to despoil the devil solely by his power and without the Passion"? If it was not so, it is because—he affirms with Saint Augustine, who furnishes here the authoritative argument—it was fitting that Christ "should vanquish the devil and deliver man, not merely by the power of the divinity, but also through the justice and humility of his Passion".[2] Favoring, in the footsteps of Saint Anselm, the concept of satisfaction,[3] he will, very clearly, present the Passion as a gratuitous and free act on the part of God, who hands over his Son for sinners, but no less gratuitous and free on the part of the Christ-Man, who offers himself as ransom for them. In his opinion, the necessity in question would be only relative, that is, deriving from a cause external to the nature of God and man, and a necessity other than a violence simply submitted to, since it was voluntarily that Jesus handed himself over to his executioners. The hypothetical necessity concerns the "suitable" — means for arriving at the goal pursued, not only in relation to us, but in relation to Christ himself and to God. Again, it is to the authority of Scripture that Saint Thomas appeals:

[2] *S. Th.* III, 46, 6 obj. et ad 3.

[3] In order to avoid the current simplifications, we will abstain here from broaching the Anselmian theory of satisfaction in itself, preferring to present it within the Thomist synthesis, which picks up its essential motif: the expiatory satisfaction is accomplished by the suffering humanity of Christ, who is the instrument and demonstration of the superabundant merciful power of God (cf. *S. Th.* III, 48, 6 ad 1; 49, 4, in particular ad 2 and 3).

it is through the self-abasement of his Passion that Christ merited the glory of the exaltation (cf. Lk 24:26); in that, he accomplishes the design of the trinitarian God proclaimed by the Law and the Prophets (cf. 24:22, 44, 46). In other words, the Passion responds essentially to a necessity contained in the free design of eternal Wisdom, who wanted to free man and to lead him to beatitude by this means and no other.

For Saint Thomas no less than for von Balthasar, the Passion is the heart of the redemptive mystery, the definitive revelation of the *mysterion* of which Saint Paul speaks in the Letter to the Ephesians (1:3ff.; cf. 3:3ff.), the salvation of mankind through the blood of the Cross. In order to explain its value, is it enough to say, like certain modern theologians, that from all eternity God chose the Cross as the definitive sign of his salvific will? Certain expressions of Aquinas are open to such an interpretation of the Passion, as when he said, for example, that man thereby "knew how much God loved him and was thereby stirred to love him in return", or again, that thereby "Christ gave us the example of obedience, humility, constancy, justice, and other virtues necessary to man's salvation."[4] The Passion would thus be a kind of "real symbolism" of saving love, an example that brings about virtue. Moreover, discussing the Resurrection of Christ, the cause of our justification, Aquinas expresses himself in terms of exemplary causality.

In his doctrine, nevertheless, this type of causality goes well beyond the symbolical order governing the relations between men; it has a truly sacramental character.[5] What is

---

[4] *S. Th.* III, 46, 3.
[5] Cf. *S. Th.* III, 56, 1 and 2; *Compendium theologiae*, 239.

emphasized in this inner-worldly sign is the properly human-divine efficacy of the unique act of the One who posits it. The Cross is the means by which God works our reconciliation, according to the words of Saint Paul: "We have redemption through his blood" (Eph 1:7). Through it, God himself acts in human nature by regenerating it from within. He, in fact, wanted, to save us, not through his will alone, but through the meritorious and atoning work of the Cross.

Before specifying the nature of the work thus described, let us pause a moment at the explanation Saint Thomas gives of the sufferings of the Passion.

According to him, Christ not only endured all sufferings (generically, not, of course, specifically), but the sufferings he endured transcended all others in intensity. Aquinas does not thereby mean that the essence of the Passion is in the number and extent of the sufferings: the "very least" of these sufferings "was sufficient", in fact, "to redeem the human race from all sins";[6] what counts is their unique intensity and depth. All the same, following the saints and mystics, the Angelic Doctor endeavors with a religious concern to depict the material character of these sufferings, seeing in them so many expressions of a kenotic love that abandons itself totally, unconditionally. But what, in his eyes, renders absolutely unique the trials inflicted on Christ is the quality of the person who submits to them. If, in conformity to the traditional Christian interpretation of Lamentations 1:12, there is no suffering that could be compared with his, it is less because of the tortures themselves, whose objec-

---

[6] *S. Th.* III, 46, 5 ad 3. On this way of "calculating" what was sufficient to save men, Father von Balthasar voices some slight reservations: *Mysterium Paschale: The Mystery of Easter*, trans. Aidan Nichols, O.P., 2nd ed. (San Francisco: Ignatius Press, 2005), pp. 134–35.

tive nature is not beyond comparison with those of others who have been crucified, than by reason of the effect they had in his soul. The latter, in fact, suggests Saint Thomas,[7] "from its interior powers, apprehended most vehemently all the causes of sadness". In addition, far from seeking to ease the inner sadness and outer suffering through reason, Christ gave himself up without defense to their domination, desiring even to "take a suffering proportionate in its intensity to the greatness of the fruit that was to result from it": man's deliverance. Finally, having freely chosen the Passion as the providential instrument of salvation, he offered himself as victim of all the sins that he had come to expiate. "Christ suffered not only because of the loss of his corporal life but also because of the sins of all others. . . . It was for the sin of all that he suffered at the same time. . . . The cause of the inner pain was all the sins of the human race, for which he made satisfaction through his sufferings; he imputed them to himself, in a way, saying with the psalm: 'verba delictorum meorum' (Ps 22[21]:2)".

In the salvific action of the Passion, Saint Thomas accords the central role to the properly human operation of Christ; and in order to explain it, he appeals to the traditional explanatory concepts of merit, satisfaction, sacrifice, and ransom, as to "so many concentric notions, superimposed by reflection on the same object, each of which brings out one aspect" without ever exhausting the comprehension of this action.[8] All together, in fact, "each because of its own signification harmonized with the others", they "try to translate in their harmonious variety, because of the analogy of

[7] *S. Th.* III, 46, 6. The quotations that follow all refer to this article.

[8] J. Rivière, *Le Dogme de la Rédemption: Étude théologique*, 3rd ed. (Paris, 1931), p. 303; cf. p. 298.

the faith, the infinite and many-sided riches of the mystery."[9]

Leaving aside for the time being the moral notion of "merit" (of which we are told that the body, in particular the suffering body, is the instrument),[10] let us say a few words of the other three notions, for it is they in particular that are at issue in von Balthasar's essay, whose originality we will, in conclusion, seek to show.

— The first of these notions, satisfaction, is inspired by the general doctrine of penance. In order to obtain the salvation that is offered him by grace, man must renounce the sin that has turned him away from God. Now this renunciation is real and efficacious only if it is inscribed in his will by an act of repentance for past sins and the intention to avoid all sin in the future. Repentance and good intentions, however, are not enough to strengthen the will in the hatred of sin, for the latter sinks its roots deep into the affectivity of man. In order to conquer sin in the flesh, a work is necessary that strikes down the sensible movements that continue to incline us toward evil. In order to uproot completely the disorder of the flesh, the sinner must perform some punishment. The latter is said to be satisfactory when it is suffered voluntarily in order to imprint in the flesh the ordination toward God that the will, renewed by divine grace, has determined.

In order to be able to apply this Christian doctrine to the work of redemption, as the long tradition of the Fathers and Doctors of the Church has done, Saint Thomas provides two further details that, in addition, indicate the analogical character of such an application. The first is that

[9] Cf. F. Bourassa, "La Satisfaction du Christ", *Sciences ecclésiastiques* 15 (1963): 351–81.

[10] *S. Th.* III, 49, 6 ad 1; cf. 19, 3.

no man simply as man could offer valid satisfaction for sin before Christ came to save him, through his Passion, from the corruption of human nature; furthermore, Christ was himself absolutely pure of any sin, and it is precisely because of his innocence that he was in a state to obtain pardon for us through the expiation of the Cross. If one seeks to express the mystery of redemption in terms of satisfaction, it is necessary to be aware of the unique and, so to speak, foundational value of what Christ did. It is because the latter made full and definitive satisfaction for our sins that he gave us—through a grace that gives rise as such to man's collaboration—the ability to make satisfaction, in our turn, through voluntary penance. The analogy of faith, in which the Aquinas discourse is situated, in itself compels us to go from the imperfect satisfaction of which the Christian has experience, especially in the sacrament of confession, to the perfect satisfaction of the one who gives it all its efficaciousness.[11]

Another element of the doctrine of penance allows him to mark the specificity of Christ's work of satisfaction, the "dilection of charity", thanks to which it is possible to make satisfaction before God "through someone other" than oneself.[12] Although man in a state of sin was incapable of making satisfaction for himself and, a fortiori, for the sin of the human race—for sin is not only a slavery with respect to the flesh, but it is also what is its root cause: an offense to God—Christ, through his Passion and by his death for us, took on himself and expiated the wrongs of all. On the Cross, he endured the punishments that could free mankind from the slavery of the flesh. Now his sufferings constitute a satisfaction that is not only sufficient but superabundant,

[11] *S. Th.* III, 1, 2 ad 2.
[12] *Contra Gentiles* III, 158.

and that for three reasons:[13] the meritorious character of the supereminent charity in virtue of which he suffered, the efficient value of the divinity united to Christ the man, and finally the properly speaking penal aspect of the pains he suffered. The punishment as such acquired its importance only in its relation with the dignity of the Divine Person and the extreme charity of Christ as man. Inserted thus into its larger christological framework, it takes on its true form of "chastisement" suffered, through obedience and love, in conformity with the trinitarian plan, for the salvation of the whole human race.

It is the same reality that another traditional notion wishes to express, the notion of sacrifice. Like satisfaction, sacrifice designates first of all the external work that Christ accomplished in his flesh on the Cross. Nevertheless, this visible sacrifice, symbolized by the prefigurative sacrifices of the Old Covenant, "is the sacrament, which is to say, the sacred sign, of the invisible sacrifice"[14] that consists in offering his spirit to God. In other words, it is the expression of the inner sentiments of a soul that wishes to please God by accomplishing what he asks. If the Passion was a true sacrifice, it is thus because the one who went through it was at once and identically the one who offered it, the victim and the priest.

Although the notion of sacrifice puts more emphasis on the positive effect of the Passion—reconciliation with God—the final hermeneutical notion that Saint Thomas proposes, that of redemption (*redemptio*), expresses the infinitely costly character of this gesture.

In order to deliver us from the captivity in which the devil held us through a just permission of God, Christ had to join us where sin had placed us and to suffer for us the

[13] Cf. *S. Th.* III, 48, 2.
[14] Cf. *S. Th.* III, 48, 3 ad 2, quoting Saint Augustine.

fate that we had merited. Through the punishment that he voluntarily endured for us, he expiated the offense of the human race and thus delivered us from the servitude of sin. In emphasizing, even more than the notion of sacrifice, the vivid character of this notion, Saint Thomas warns us against too literal a use of the elements that it contains. To whom, in fact, could Christ pour out the price of our salvation? Not, certainly, to the devil, who could have no rights over sinners. Thus to God. And yet man never ceased to be subject, as creatures, to his power; it is even the Father who, through love, handed over Christ for our salvation and who thus, in a way, pays this price.[15] Now how are we to "pay" for something that belongs to us? It is advisable to retain from the image of ransoming only the elements that allow us to explain the *veritas,* the reality toward which it is directed, which Aquinas does by bringing back once again the different dimensions of the redemptive act.[16] In this act, the immediate author is the Christ-Man who has poured out his own blood, his life, in ransom for us. This life, however, is dependent on the three Divine Persons who inspired him to suffer and "paid" through his intermediation the price of the redemption. The first and remote efficient cause of salvation is thus the trinitarian God; its immediate and next cause is the Christ-Man who acted through obedience and love by offering himself as propitiatory victim for sins in conformity to the divine plan.

In order to grasp the exact significance that Thomas gives to the expiation of the Cross, we need only refer to his commentary on 2 Corinthians 5:21: "For our sake he made him to be sin." He presents three complementary explanations of this much debated scriptural passage:[17]

[15] *S. Th.* III, 48, 5 ad 2; cf. 47, 3 ad 3.
[16] Cf. *S. Th.* III, 48, 5.
[17] *Super Epist. ad Cor. 2am,* lect. V, no. 201. The last of these explanations is

1. God made him to be sin in the sense that he wanted him to be considered a sinner by popular opinion. The commentary echoes Isaiah 53:12 ("he was numbered with the transgressors") by stressing the innocence of Christ.

2. God made him to be sin in the sense that he had him assume mortal and passible flesh, similar to that of sin, in conformity with Romans 8:3 ("He sent his own Son in the likeness of sinful flesh"); the commentary this time marks the kenotic aspect of the Incarnation; nevertheless, he still does not furnish here any more than in the preceding an adequate explanation of the sufferings of the Cross.

3. It is in the third commentary, invoking Hosea 4:8 to that effect, that Saint Thomas expresses something of the specific character of the latter. The explanation rests on the distinction, introduced by Saint Hilary, between the *sensus poenae* and the *vis poenae*, which Saint Ambrose sets forth by arguing: "Pietatis est susceptio peccatorum ista, non criminis" (it is the property of piety to assume sins, not crime).[18] In this sense, Saint Thomas will not refuse to say that Christ experienced the *malum* (*sensus*) *poenae*, clearly distinguishing the latter from the *malum culpae*, which Ambrose calls the *vis poenae*: "The curse of sin is one thing, which is far from Christ; something else is the punishment Christ suffered voluntarily when he was made a curse, or sin, for us, that is to say, victim for sin, so as to lift the curse from all, that of the sin and that of the punishment."[19] Since sin is an act originating in the will, the *malum culpae* or the *vis*

---

that which Aquinas also proposes in relation to Galatians 3:13: "He became a curse for us"; see on this subject: *S. Th.* III, 46, 4 ad 3.

[18] *In Ps* 37:6.

[19] *Quaestiones et decisiones in epist. ad Gal.*, in PL 175:559 (text wrongly attributed to Hugh of Saint-Victor) and *Super Epist. ad Gal.*, lect. V, nos. 148–49.

poenae cannot be attributed to Christ, whose soul is pure of any malice, except by an external attribution: insofar as he was considered an iniquitous sinner. Men judged him to be such, but in reality Jesus bore the punishment for our sins; his passible and mortal body, in the likeness of sinful flesh, and, more specifically still, the sufferings of the Cross were the instrument and, as it were, the matter God used in order to effect our salvation. As for Christ, he assumed the curse of punishment freely, through love, in order to redeem us both from sin and from the punishment of sin.

Aquinas does not go so far as to speak, as von Balthasar tends to do, of an exchange between the sinless Son of God and sinful man, for in his eyes and for the Fathers of the Church, there could be no intimate contact between the Immaculate One and the universe of sin. Would not such an affirmation lead to the heretical position of someone like Luther, for whom Christ was made a curse and sin because he assumed the person of the sinner? While stressing, through images that are necessarily inadequate for comprehending such a mystery, that Christ suffered the most profound sadness in absolute measure, that the weight of the Cross, even more spiritual than corporal, is out of proportion to common strength, superhuman in the strongest sense of the word, Saint Thomas nevertheless sets limits to this suffering: the latter did not go beyond the "rule of reason"; and it cannot in any way be compared to that of the separated soul, for damnation "transcends all the evils of this life". Moreover, he believes it necessary to add, "innocence diminishes the number of sufferings: for if the guilty suffers not only from the punishment but also from the fault, the innocent endures only the pain of the punishment." In this sense, the reparation that the Just One provides remains external with respect to the offense committed. Of course, the pain "grows in him because of his innocence the more he grasps that the punishment that provokes it is unmerited." But, as he specifies farther on: "The higher reason, in Christ, did not suffer thereby on the part of its object, which is God, for God was the cause, not of grief, but rather of delight and joy for the soul of Christ" in its higher part.[20] While Christ suffered in his body and in the inferior powers of his soul, notwithstanding these sufferings, he enjoyed the beatific vision perfectly. The cry of abandonment that the Gospels report (Mt 27:46 and Mk 15:34) thus does not mean, as Saint Ambrose suggests, that "the divinity withdrew" from the one who was in the process of dying; rather, it means quite simply that God "exposed Christ to the power of his persecutors".[21] While noting that the Passion is the deed of his Divine Person itself, Aquinas refuses to attribute to the latter an inner sense of the divinity itself, for "the Word, remaining God by nature, is impassible."[22] Totally unfamiliar with the questions modern psychology poses and a contemporary theology develops, concerned to place in evidence the humanly existential character of the Passion, the Angelic Doctor endeavors above all to safeguard one essential given of the Christian faith: at no moment of his life did the incarnate Word cease to be ontologically united to God, since he is God in Person.

In an extreme position justified by none of the scriptural witnesses, Luther went so far as to declare Christ "damned". Careful not to cross such a line himself, von Balthasar nevertheless tries to transcend the extrinsicism of the traditional Thomist solution, in which the offense and reparation for the offense remain exterior to each other. Christ, he goes

[20] *S. Th.* III, 46, 7. Cf. III, 46, 8.
[21] *S. Th.* III, 47, 3; cf. 50, 2 obj. 1.
[22] *S. Th.* III, 46, 12.

on to explain, knew himself to be charged with an absolutely unique mission, comprising the task of suffering and dying for others and demanding that he freely assume the inner condition of the sinner. In order to join the latter in his own freedom, the undertaking in his favor must in fact take place, according to him, there in the very place where the refusal and curse took place. In order to grasp the true significance of the suggested solution, a few words on the consciousness of Jesus are necessary. And first of all, what the most recent exegetes and theologians say about it.

The "Pro Nobis" in the Consciousness of Jesus

If, during the Passion, Christ experienced, in his whole soul, what Saint Thomas Aquinas called the *fruitio beata*, the blessed fruition, can we attribute to the experience of Calvary all the seriousness involved, to the contrary, in the past and present tragedy of so many men and women crushed not only physically but psychologically in concentration and torture camps?[1] Does not such a theory risk disqualifying, in the eyes of our contemporaries, the mystery of the Cross such as the Church has continually proclaimed it since Pentecost (cf. Acts 2:14–26)? And how could Christians themselves remain convinced of the affliction of the One who "although he was a Son, . . . learned obedience through what he suffered" (Heb 5:8), becoming "obedient unto death, even death on a cross" (Phil 2:8), if theologians explain to them that, unlike other men, Jesus, in the midst of his suf-

[1] On the blessed fruition, see *S. Th.* III, 46, 8. Armed with this concept, the Holy Office, on June 5, 1918, condemned the following proposition: "It is not certain that there was in the soul of Christ, while he was living among men, the knowledge possessed by the blessed or those who have the beatific vision" (DH 3645). The question, difficult to evade today, that is raised by such a teaching is expressed in the sarcastic comments of B. Besret, who reports the following anecdote: "A parish priest asks children: What did Jesus say on the Cross? A kid replies: He said: I don't care, since I'm going to be resurrected on the third day anyway!" (*De commencement en commencement: Itinéraire d'une déviance* [Paris, 1967], p. 167).

ferings, did not cease to find in God a source of delight and joy?

Of course, these same theologians could rightly object, the assertions of Aquinas like the declarations of the Magisterium that tend in the same direction must not be interpreted in a unilateral way. Thus, when the former says that the soul of Christ, during the Passion, entirely enjoyed the beatific vision, that does not mean, they clarify with subtlety, that such a vision was entirely beatific.[2] Likewise, from another viewpoint, when, in the encyclical *Mystici Corporis*, Pius XII affirms that, thanks to this vision, Christ possessed a knowledge of all the members of his Mystical Body,[3] he probably does not intend to pronounce a judgment thereby on the fullness of the knowledge that his human intellect had at that time.[4] But explanations of this kind scarcely make the central mystery of the Credo more accessible to believers: the suffering of Christ as a substitution that makes amends for the sins of all mankind—"crucifixus etiam pro nobis".

---

[2] "It is one thing to say that the vision of the divine essence remained during the most profound throes of the Cross; it is something else to say that it was entirely beatific. It did not in fact affect the lower powers that Jesus fully abandoned to their natural objects and to all the causes of suffering. But . . . Saint Thomas clarifies that the soul itself, being by its essence the form of the body, was the subject of the Passion while it was also the subject of beatitude. It is the same being that at once suffers and enjoys" (M.-J. Nicolas, in Thomas Aquinas, *Somme théologique*, vol. 4 [Paris, 1986], p. 343).

[3] DH 3812.

[4] According to C. Duquoc, "the decisions of the Magisterium have never wished to impose a theological tradition in that area", and "the pope here was merely repeating a theology that was widespread at the time" (*Christologie: Essai dogmatique*, vol. 2, *L'Homme Jésus* [Paris, 1968], pp. 160–61). J. Collantes expresses himself in more nuanced terms on this point: *La fede della Chiesa cattolica: Le idee e gli uomini nei documenti dottrinali del Magistero* (Vatican, 1993), pp. 275–76.

On the contrary, by attributing to him an awareness shielded from uncertainties, doubts, anguish, in brief, from what is an essential mark of our mortal condition, they risk reinforcing the opinion of those who, on the basis of any other theological presuppositions, deny, by the test of the Cross, the at once fully human and unique, incomparable appropriateness of a salvific event that concerns creation as a whole.

That the unspeakable experience of the Cross such as Jesus lived it in his earthly existence is the central mystery of the faith is a fact that popular piety and the ecclesial sense have always spontaneously held to be indisputable. But with the progress of exegetical works, the relation between the Jesus of history going toward his death and the risen Christ such as the early Christians confessed him has become problematical. The gap opened by early investigations, from Harnack to Bultmann, on the historicity of the earthly Jesus even seemed, early on, to be impossible to bridge. Bultmann writes:

> If one seeks to reconstruct the character of Jesus, we are placed in the greatest dilemma by the fact that we cannot know how Jesus understood his end, understood his death. . . . It is difficult to understand this execution as the intrinsically necessary consequence of his action; on the contrary, it happened through a kind of misunderstanding of his action as being political action. It would then be, from a historical point of view, a senseless fate. Did he find sense in it? And if so, what? We cannot know. It is not permissible to conceal the possibility that Jesus came to nothing.[5]

---

[5] *Das Verhältnis der urchristlichen Christusbotschaft zum historischen Jesus*, 2nd ed. (Heidelberg, 1961), p. 12. The author did not intend by this hypothesis so much to supply a solution as to challenge the superficial assurance that a naively biographical conception of the life of Jesus could furnish.

There has been no shortage of Catholic exegetes following him to endorse, in more measured terms, this questioning that challenges the naive certitudes of the past.

"The Gospels", explains A. George in a journal with a large readership, "relate to us few words of Jesus about himself and his mission. . . . They were written in the Church in the light of the Paschal revelation. We can wonder if this concern did not lead them to emphasize Jesus' announcements of his Passion, to make these announcements more specific 'ex eventu', also to mix a theological interpretation with them?"[6]

According to a French exegete, if we examine the Gospel of Mark, we obtain at the very most the image of a stoic hero:

> All things considered, Mark's account presents a lucid man who goes to a death that he has foreseen but that he goes through in an inner rending, in solitude from his own people and hostility from others; a fully human being, in the maximum stress of suffering; but also in the absolute greatness of freedom. What characterizes Jesus is not only the lucidity with which he sees his death approaching or the courage with which he confronts it, it is the meaning that he gives to his death: he makes of his death an act of his mission; he transcends as an offering this death that is imposed on him; he denounces the crime of guilty men at the very moment when he reads this death proclaimed by the Scriptures in the plan of God.[7]

With the post-Bultmannians themselves, we fortunately witnessed afterward a reevaluation of the history of Jesus

---

[6] "Comment Jésus a-t-il perçu sa propre mort?" *Lumière et Vie* vol. 20, no. 101 (1971): 34.

[7] L. Chordat, *Jésus devant sa mort dans l'évangile de Marc* (Paris, 1970), pp. 106–7.

in relation to ecclesial faith, which von Balthasar, in line
with the Second Vatican Council,[8] greets favorably and from
which he seeks to draw the essential teaching.

The question that his first conference raises in this context
is that of knowing if, during his earthly life, Jesus was aware
of being the true Son of God (cf. 2 Pet 1:16–18), charged
with a mission of universal dimensions: that of reconciling
the entire world with God through the Cross (cf. 2 Cor
5:19), and if he gave his death the meaning of a free act of
love in substitution for sinners.

Of course, he willingly concedes to Father Léon-Dufour
and other scholars of historico-critical exegesis, it is permis-
sible to doubt that Christ expressly pronounced certain particularly explicit words reported by the Gospels. Would not
attributing to him, for example, the words of Mark 10:45:
"*lytron* [ransom] for many" lead to making him, as the French
Jesuit says, "a theoretician of his existence"? But that does
not mean that he did not know, from the first dawning of his
human consciousness, his profound identity and the unique
mission that had been confided to him. For such is indeed
the conviction of von Balthasar.

In support of this, he could cite here Father J. Guillet:
"If the person of Jesus is to be the Son of God, he must be
so, from his birth, as soon as he exists, otherwise he would
never be so. [Moreover] he must be so, and he must know it,
for no one can teach that to him. . . . No human word, even
the finest and most precise, can bring that lived experience
which is that of being God."[9] He might also have referred

---

[8] Cf. *Dei Verbum*, no. 19.

[9] *Jésus devant sa vie et sa mort* (Paris, 1971), p. 56. On the development of
Jesus' human consciousness, Guillet relates a particularly penetrating reflection by M. Blondel.

to the study of H. Schürmann,[10] who, rather than discussing things Jesus said about his death, pays particular attention to what he calls the *ipsissima facta* and, through them, to the fundamental demand inspiring his life and mission, and in particular the gestures performed during the Paschal meal. On the question that concerns us, according to the German Catholic exegete, there are positive reasons to think that the pre-Paschal *hyper* did not remain purely implicit: not only did Jesus foresee his death and personally attribute to it a specific meaning, but, later at the Last Supper, he indicated to the limited circle of his disciples the meaning and value of it for the salvation of the world.

Von Balthasar did not fail to state his thinking on this point with some specificity, carefully examining the most outstanding exegetical analyses and theological positions on the subject.[11] In his Parisian conferences, he was content to state his concept succinctly, differentiating it, not without the inevitable simplifications, with respect to that of one or another author known to his public. The thesis he supports is entirely in line with the direction of the great tradition of the mystics and saints: Jesus was conscious of the universal meaning of his mission, and the Pauline texts on the *pro nobis* (1 Cor 15:3-5 and passim) only make explicit the meaning of a historical event whose dramatic character he

---

[10] *Comment Jésus a-t-il vécu sa mort* (Paris, 1977), in particular the chapter "Comment Jésus a-t-il affronté sa mort", pp. 21-81.

[11] Let us point out, in addition to *Mysterium Paschale*, already mentioned: *The Glory of the Lord: A Theological Aesthetics*, vol. 7, *Theology: The New Covenant*, trans. Brian McNeil, C.R.V. (San Francisco: Ignatius Press, 1989), pp. 202-35; and especially, *Theo-Drama: Theological Dramatic Theory*, vol. 4: *The Action*, trans. Graham Harrison (San Francisco: Ignatius Press, 1994), pp. 231-423.

himself experienced in his flesh. The salvific meaning of the
death of Christ is a given of the gospel proclamation prior
to Paul (cf. Rom 6:3): it was part of the earliest Credo, the
very one from which our formula would develop: "propter
nos homines et propter nostram salutem. . . ." This meaning is that which Jesus gave to it historically and that he
alone could confer on it, in conformity with the unicity
of his person and his mission. The theologian insists on
it: the substitution that Paul describes is not the result of a
belated New Testament soteriology. The way in which the
early Church interpreted the life, death, and Resurrection
of Christ corresponds to that of which Jesus himself was
aware and what he explained when he said farewell to his
disciples.

On this point, von Balthasar differentiates himself absolutely from those who, because of the results of some
historico-critical exegesis, believe it necessary to relativize
the value of the Pauline affirmations, seeing in them the expression of a late New Testament soteriology, thereby plac-
ing in doubt the fact that Christ offered himself with the idea
of an expiatory sacrifice. According to K. Rahner, whom he
has particularly in view here: "the . . . question whether the
pre-resurrection Jesus himself already interpreted his death
explicitly as an 'expiatory sacrifice' for the world" must remain open from a historical point of view. In the view of
the German theologian, it is prudent to confine ourselves
here to a "minimal assertion": Jesus considers the death to
which he freely went as being part of his destiny as prophet,
included in the merciful plan of God. "Jesus maintains in
death his unique claim of an identity between his message
and his person in the hope that in this death he will be
vindicated by God with regard to his claim." On the other
hand, as far as the Pauline doctrine of redemption is con-

cerned, it is a "legitimate but secondary interpretation" of the irreversible victory of God in the world, made manifest historically in the death and Resurrection of Jesus.[12]

If Rahner was careful not to call into question the theological meaning of the death of Jesus as expiatory sacrifice, other theologians scarcely hesitated to take the plunge. The first names to which von Balthasar referred in this respect were those of his compatriot H. Küng and the Belgian Dominican E. Schillebeeckx, the two theologians who, several months before the conference he held in Paris, had both been questioned by the Congregation for the Doctrine of the Faith. He mentions them three times, but in passing, less to make a proper critique of them than to illustrate his own thought by contrasting it to them.

In order to discover "who is Christ", the author of *On Being a Christian* questions the New Testament by taking

[12] *Foundations of Christian Faith*, trans. William V. Dych (New York: Crossroad, 1984), pp. 254–55. Cf. E. Maurice, *La Christologie de Karl Rahner* (Paris, 1995), p. 193. Balthasar devoted a long critical analysis to the soteriology of K. Rahner in *Theo-Drama* 3:273–84. In his work *Le Dieu Trinité dans l'histoire: Le différend théologique Balthasar-Rahner* (Paris, 1995), V. Holzer scarcely approaches *in recto* the soteriological question. Examining the two theologians from the point of view of an "aesthetical Christology" (p. 365; cf. pp. 431ff.), he believes he is able to identify two different and, in the end, irreducible logics in them. It could be questioned whether the point of departure of his inquiry is sufficiently sound. What the author calls the aesthetical Christology of Balthasar (referring to *The Glory of the Lord* in the French edition, *La Gloire et la Croix*, vol. 1 [Paris, 1990], pp. 387–88) is more precisely, in our opinion, an "eidetic Christology", consisting in the application to Christology of an a priori methodology that is less formal-structural than phenomenological in nature (cf. *Glory of the Lord*, 7:14–15). The theological aesthetic, which Balthasar distinguishes carefully from aesthetical theology, is "the reception, solely in a perception of faith, of the sovereignly free divine love and of his glory in its self-explanatory movement" (*Glaubhaft is nur Liebe* [Einsiedeln, 1963, 5th ed., 1985], p. 6).

up again, with slight differences, the thesis of one of Bult-mann's predecessors, Martin Kähler, according to whom the precious historical memories contained in the Gospels do not give access to the true Christ, the one of the Church's confession of faith. In Jesus of Nazareth, Küng sees above all the individual in history who claimed to be the representative of God and men, prompting his contemporaries to an ultimate decision in favor of the good news he was announcing. His violent death was, according to him, "the logical consequence of his attitude toward God and men";[13] "the movement that claims to represent him really appeared only after [his] death."[14]

As for the theologian from Nijmegen, he tends, in the same sense, to reduce the *pro nobis* of the early Credo to the "historical intention" that characterized Jesus' behavior up

---

[13] *Vingt propositions de "Être chrétien"* (Paris, 1979), p. 44.

[14] Ibid., p. 47. Von Balthasar proved very early on to be highly critical with respect to Hans Küng. After a brief period when a collaboration seemed to be beginning—in 1966, he entrusted to him the publication of his theological meditations on eschatological expectation (*Zuerst Gottes Reich*)—he wrote, in 1968, a very severe review of his work on the Church (in *Civitas* 23:450–53). Two years after the publication of *On Being a Christian*, he entered into an open discussion with the author in an essay entitled "Crucified for Us" ("Gekreuzigt für uns: 'Um unserer Sünden willen hingeopfert' [Rom 4:25]", in *Diskussion über Hans Küngs "Christ sein"* [Mainz, 1976], pp. 83–92). This essay is certainly in the background of the remarks in the present essay. Two years later, he wrote again on the subject of the theologian from Lucerne "A Letter to a Fellow-Priest" (in *Boletín Eclesiástico de Filipinas* 52, no. 578 [January 1978]: pp. 62–67). Then, in 1979, he wrote in the local journals a response to accusations launched against the "Superstar Wojtyla". At the time when Küng saw the title of Catholic theologian withdrawn, von Balthasar considered once again the positions of his compatriot (an English translation of his speech, which appeared in the *Frankfurter Allgemeine Zeitung*, was published in *Communio: International Catholic Review* 5/1 [1980]: 91–93).

to his death. According to him, the only thing that exegesis permits us to affirm is that "Jesus sensed his death as [in some way] involved in salvation on the part of God, as a historical consequence of his service, zealous with love and solidarity toward men."[15] This would be far from Jesus willing his death as a determining factor of salvation; it would cast the shadow of myth over his action on behalf of men; the pre-Paschal Jesus would see in it a historical element of his global mission of salvation "as a consequence of the rejection of his preaching and his conduct".[16]

In his first conference, von Balthasar prefers to quote French-language theologians, more familiar to his audience, like, for example, Father J. Galot and Father J. Moingt. In the meantime, the latter has published, besides, a large work taking up and developing the 1976 contribution that, in the present volume, serves to illustrate the reduction of the *pro nobis* to human solidarity. In fact, Moingt, for his part, excludes the thought that Jesus offers himself in reparation for our sins, finding the idea of an effective human solidarity sufficient. "The death of Christ", he explains, "is not the expiation of sin that he suffered in our place"; "his death does not redeem, one by one, the sins of all men taken individually",[17] otherwise it would not be the revelation of the perfectly disinterested love of God. According to the Jesuit theologian, the pre-Paschal Jesus is a model for us of filial freedom:

> He seeks his Father beyond the God of his fathers, a Father whom he does not receive from others but whom he gives to them, "my Father"; he goes off to discover a new face of the Wholly Other God, full of assurance, though he

---

[15] *Jezus het verhaal van een levende*, 2nd ed. (Bloemendaal, 1974), p. 255.

[16] Ibid., p. 251; cf. p. 256.

[17] *L'Homme qui venait de Dieu* (Paris, 1999), pp. 538–39.

ventures on a path that is solitary and not opened up in advance, destitute of the security and assistance of the tradition of ancestors and a common knowledge, running the risk of being denounced as an enemy of the law of his people; and when his approach is effectively condemned as blasphemy by the higher authorities to whom God has confided this people, although he could have escaped danger by protesting that he wanted to destroy nothing of the prerogatives of the Temple, he prefers to confront death rather than to seem to contradict his past teachings; he does not fear to suffer the worst death there is before God, that of a blasphemer. He overcomes the death he suffers; he dismisses it by going ahead of it; he abandons himself to it by sovereignly asserting himself; he suffers his destiny by leading it himself to its end. He thus achieves the perfect freedom of the man faced with death and faced with God, faced with a death inflicted in the name of God.[18]

That death he accepted in a feeling of dereliction accompanied by a sincere desire of disinterested abandonment of self to God; he gave with the witness of his blood an attestation of the gratuitous gift of God with respect to the world, "a gesture of solidarity and liberation that extended and bound him forever to all mankind".[19]

Quite different is the image of Jesus that von Balthasar depicts in fidelity to his phenomenological method, substantially inspired by Pierre Rousselot and his doctrine of the *Eyes of Faith* (1910).[20] In order to grasp that image in its truth, we must, according to him, see it and understand it as the Church presents it to us: as the human-divine figure of revelation, which demands and at the same time, of course, presupposes, on our part, faith in his divinity. This

[18] Ibid., p. 540.
[19] Ibid., p. 541.
[20] Cf. *Glory of the Lord*, 1:175–77.

central figure in which all revelation is concentrated in fact appears only to the eyes of the heart, illuminated by grace (Eph 1:18), because only the "simple eye" (Mt 6:22) is capable of perceiving in it what it wishes to express: the ultimate manifestation of God in his unfathomable mystery of love. The author explains that through a still approximate comparison:

> Just as a natural form—a flower, for instance—can be seen for what it is only when it is perceived and "received" as the appearance of a certain depth of life, so, too, Jesus' form can be seen for what it is only when it is grasped and accepted as the appearance of a divine depth transcending all worldly nature. Moreover, in view of the nature of the reality involved, the human beholder can be brought to such perception only by the grace of God, that is, by a participation in this same depth that makes him proportionate to the wholly new dimension of a form-phenomenon which comprises within itself both God and world.[21]

If, in conformity with the unanimous attestation of the New Testament, the Church has understood the suffering of Christ as a redemptive "substitution", it was necessary that Jesus, too, be aware of it. To affirm the contrary would mean, for von Balthasar, dislocating the givens of revelation. One could, in the spirit of his method, paint a portrait of Jesus showing the awareness he had of representing, in his existence, the ultimate commitment of God on behalf of men. Let us briefly sketch such a portrait, based on the interpretation that Saint Paul gives of the life, death, and Resurrection of Jesus Christ, in conformity with the Gospel proclamation of which he himself was one of the first beneficiaries: "He died for all, that those who live might live no

[21] Ibid., 153–54.

longer for themselves but for him who for their sake died and was raised" (2 Cor 5:15; cf. Rom 6:11).

To God who "so loved the world that he gave his . . . Son" for us (Jn 3:16), the latter responds by voluntarily giving himself. The coming of Christ Jesus into the world in order to save it from sin and death seems to be both a free act and a supreme testimony of love toward his Father. It is in fact freely that the Son gives his life to men (cf. Jn 10:18; 12:27, and the prophecy of Is 53:7), and he accomplishes this gesture through gratitude to the One who "loves [him] and has given all things into his hand" (Jn 3:35). It is because of his Father that he loves men so much and gives up his life for them "to the end" (Jn 13:1). He knows that the Cross will be for them an inexhaustible source of love; he also knows that his death for them anticipates the secret desire of the Father: "For this reason the Father loves me, because I lay down my life, that I may take it again" (Jn 10:17); "I always do what is pleasing to him" (Jn 8:29). His consolation is to love the Father by totally doing his will and by loving men, since the Father loves men. The Incarnation—up to its ultimate consequences[22]—was decided upon between them in love. The Holy Spirit, who was the irrevocable witness to this joint decision, in a way guaranteed the accomplishment of it. "I said: 'Behold, I have come to do your will, O God'"; and so, through the power of the Holy Spirit, "a body have you prepared for me" as

---

[22] The Fathers have more than once stressed the ordination of the Incarnation to the Passion: "If the flesh was not to be saved, the Word of God would not have been made flesh, and, if the blood of the just were not to be accounted for, the Lord would not have had blood" (Irenaeus, *Against Heresies* V, 14, 1). Cf. Among many other witnesses: Athanasius, *Oratio de Incarnatione Verbi* 44 (PG 25:173C–176B).

a "sin offering" (Heb 10:5ff., quoting and commenting on
Ps 40:7–9).

The very core of the will of Christ on earth is nothing
else but love and the joy contained in the love of being able
to serve the Father by making himself the Servant of men.
Yet, the closer "the hour" comes when he is going to "give
himself as a ransom for all" (1 Tim 2:6; cf. Mt 20:28), the
more "trouble" (Jn 11:33; 12:27; 13:21) and even "distress
and trouble" (Mk 14:33) are going to invade his soul. Increasingly his mission of love will take on the characteris-
tics of a hard "obedience" (Rom 5:19), a completely naked
obedience, stripped of the consolations that love provides.
From the beginning of his ministry, Jesus lives in the perspective of the hour of his return to the Father (cf. Jn 16:28):
he knows with certainty that the hour must come and that
it will be a severe trial. Yet he does not anticipate it (cf.
Jn 7:30; 8:20), even when, at the entreaty of his Mother,
he reveals symbolically the meaning and efficacy of it (cf.
Jn 2:1ff.). He leaves the decision entirely to the Father, renouncing the knowledge that falls to him as God (cf. Mk
13:32). Of himself, he makes no plan, he sets no personal
norm or ideal for himself. The only "rule" he wishes to obey
is the one dictated at every instant and in ever unexpected
ways by the Holy Spirit, who represents for him the will of
the Father. He docilely allows himself to be led by him in
all his actions (cf., for example, Lk 4:1, 14, 18), and even
in his innermost feelings, there is nothing that is not the
fruit of a wholly filial obedience (cf. Lk 10:21). In him, that
obedience is not reduced to accepting the material circum-
stances of existence; it embraces his whole person, his faith,
his love, his prayer, and his most secret thoughts—which
he does not "produce" but, rather, receives in a perfectly

transparent availability. At every moment, he is ready to respond to the external or internal promptings of the Spirit
who directs his life in the name of his Father.

When at last he recognizes, through the prophetic gesture of Mary of Bethany (cf. Jn 12:3ff.), that "the hour has
come for the Son of man to be glorified" (Jn 12:23), he sur-
renders himself completely to this hour (cf. Jn 12:27; 13:1;
16:32; 17:1) in an abandonment that is going to take him
to the most extreme humiliation. Up until then, he had indeed come up against sin through the sometimes hardened
sinners he encountered on his path. But this sin is imposed
on him now in all the horror of its anonymity: no longer
the sin of such and such a person whom he loves and whom
he has come to save, but sin as such from the "whole world
[that] is in the power of the Evil One" (1 Jn 5:19). So,
in the final analysis, the hour is revealed to be completely
different, infinitely more difficult than anything he could
have imagined. And the Father does nothing apparently to
withdraw from him the anguish that floods his heart. The
redemptive plan that had been decided in the communion
of love is accomplished in the most painful separation: the
Holy Spirit no longer seems to have any function but that
of stretching to the maximum the bonds that eternally unite
the Father and the Son. The relation of love between God
and his Christ, whom "he made . . . to be sin" (1 Cor 5:21;
cf. Rom 8:3; Gal 3:13), henceforth assumes "the form of dis-
pleasure, where the one is a stranger to the other".[23]

At Gethsemane, the Son renounces through love the use
of his human will, insofar as the latter might contrast with
that of the Father (cf. Mk 14:36), who is "greater than [he]"

---

[23] *Nouveaux points de repère*, p. 221.

(Jn 14:28), and he receives in return, with gratitude, a will wholly penetrated with the very will of the Father. On the Cross, to which he is nailed, his body is incapable henceforth of moving, surrendered, naked, to the will of his executioners: he loses any possibility of control, even over the sufferings to which he nevertheless "thirsts" (Jn 19:28; cf. Mk 10:39) to submit for the redemption of the world. He lets himself be taken to the slaughterhouse like a lamb (cf. Jn 1:29; Is 53:7), without understanding or knowing any longer what he is—"worm" or "man" (Ps 22:6)—by putting himself unreservedly in the hands of the One who has ceased to show him his face (cf. Mk 15:34). He is no longer anything but the corporal execution of his mission. Then it is death and the "descent into hell" (cf. Acts 2:31; Rom 10:7; Eph 4:8–10; 1 Pet 3:19). The love of filial obedience makes possible in Christ a state in which, without ratifying sin's No to God, the one who is pure is plunged into the anti-world of the impure, into the "objective reality" of hell, which he experiences in an exclusive and unique manner, and not only inclusively, as do sinners. In fact, as the theologian De Bâle again explains in interpreting the statements of Adrienne von Speyr, "his experience of the abyss is at the same time entirely within him (inasmuch as he assumes in himself the full measure of the mortal sinners' estrangement with respect to God) and also entirely outside himself, for this experience is for him (insofar as eternal Son of the Father) something entirely foreign: he is on Holy Saturday in perfect alienation to himself."[24]

---

[24] "Descente aux enfers", in *Axes* (1970), p. 8. (See Hans Urs von Balthasar, "Descent into Hell", in *Spirit and Institution*, trans. Edward T. Oakes, S.J., Explorations in Theology, vol. 4 [San Francisco: Ignatius Press, 1995], p. 411.)

A perfect unity, of course, exists between the active life of Jesus and the Passion. But by stressing continuity unilaterally, for instance by using the notion of solidarity with sinners, we risk, according to von Balthasar, losing sight of the clear break marked by "the hour" in the Gospel of Saint John.[25]

Jesus, in presenting himself to his people during the three years of his public life, supported by an extraordinary claim about himself, could not have been unaware of what so unique a mission entailed as consequences for his own life. He knew that he would have to pay for such a claim, even if, because of his obedience to the mission, he probably did not allow himself to examine the nature of those consequences. Before the moment of the Passion arrived, it is probable that he envisaged death as the inevitable consequence of this mission, without, for all that, experiencing the need to consider reflexively the relationship with the content of the good news of the kingdom that he was proclaiming. Like K. Rahner and, moreover, Saint Thomas Aquinas himself,[26] von Balthasar sees in the obedience of Jesus an essential trait of his earthly life (cf. Lk 2:51). Nevertheless, unlike the former, he refuses to deny him the awareness of the redemptive meaning of his suffering and death: the explanations with which Jesus accompanies the institution of the Eucharist shows that he is going to the Passion knowing the unique significance of this ultimate act in his mission as

[25] The author bases his interpretation here on the studies of R. Schnackenburg and A. George (in particular in "L'Heure de Jean XVII", in *Rev. Bibl.* 61 [1954]: 392–97).

[26] The fact that, because of the hypostatic union, Jesus possessed an infused knowledge does not exclude in any way, as Aquinas specifies in *S. Th.* III, 12, 2, that there was also in him an acquired knowledge, obtained as in every man through the active intellect that draws knowledge from the imagination.

Savior. The Cross is not only the "real symbol" (*Realsymbol*) of God's salvific love: it is not enough to declare that Jesus freely accepts death as a sign effectively demonstrating the intensity of God's love for mankind. If, in the name of that love, one rejects the idea of anger in God, thinking that God has always been reconciled with mankind, one cancels out what Scripture says of his inexorable judgment about sin (cf. Heb 4:11; 10:31, and passim).

At the end of his apostolic life, in the Passion, he, the Pure One, the "being for us" of God that he knew he represented, handed himself over without defense to us, the "faithless" (2 Tim 2:13), which means for him, von Balthasar interprets, freely subjecting himself to the "consuming fire" (Heb 12:29) through obedient love of the Father and of sinful men. The attributes of God are no less wrath than love; the divine holiness cannot, in fact, not annihilate all that is impure. The motive for which Jesus voluntarily hands himself over to death for all sinners is much more than a simple solidarity; it is, in his eyes, a human-divine love that impels him to allow universal sin to be concentrated in his person so that the separation between sin and sinner might be effected in it and, through it, in us, in conformity with the mysterious assertion of Saint Paul: "For our sake he made him to be sin [not sinner!] who knew no sin, so that in him we might become the [salvific] righteousness of God" (2 Cor 5:21). For sin, the object of divine wrath (1 Thess 2:16), came to dwell in the beloved man, and in order to extirpate it from his heart, Christ accomplished a gesture of substitution that is much more than a purely juridical transfer: it is, in the consciousness of the one who posits it, an act that leads him to experience most intimately the offense, the deficiency of the other, in order to remove from him that deficiency.

To this end, von Balthasar again explains, "it is on the very

site of the one who says No, of his unhappiness and his fall,
that the one must be placed who wishes to commit himself
totally for him."[27] Knowing that he has come to fulfill in
an absolutely transcendent way the figure of the Suffering
Servant on whom "the Lord has laid the iniquity of us all"
(Is 53:12), Jesus sees the self-offering in death as the result
of the mission he received from his Father. In order for the
substitution in question to be effected in truth, "it was necessary", adds the theologian, "that he set himself this task
consciously" and that, at the same time, inextricably, he no
longer perceive it except in an inner night that includes—
according to Adrienne von Speyr, whose testimony stands
out here as one of other mystics—"the sense of collapse
into non-meaning".[28]

This long development on the *pro nobis* in the consciousness of Jesus was necessary so as to avoid resolutely an interpretation that reduces the Cross to a purely symbolic action.
Christ goes consciously and freely to his death, understanding it in advance as an expiatory act of love in substitution
for sinners. The Passion is not a simple demonstration of the
salvific will of God; it is the completely real implementation
of that will. The act of love in regard to God and men by
means of which the latter is accomplished is, in Jesus, an act
of obedience brought to life by a sovereign decision: "No
one takes [my life] from me," he declares, "but I lay it down

[27] " 'Cruxifixus etiam pro nobis' Le mystère de la substitution", in: *Nouveaux points de repère* (Paris, 1980), p. 214 (published for the first time in *Communio* 5/1 [1980], pp. 52–62, here, p. 56). To the objection of Schillebeeckx
concerning Jesus' commitment in his apostolic action, Balthasar responds by
invoking the example of the Old Testament prophets: they show, he explains,
that it is "perfectly possible to be committed with all one's powers to a work
that one knows in the final analysis one will not be able to bring to a successful
end" (*Nouveaux points de repère*, p. 214).

[28] Ibid., pp. 215–16.

of my own accord" (Jn 10:18). Understood in the light of
these words, the *pro nobis* permits us to reject at the same
stroke exegesis that sees in the Cross the punishment of an
innocent in place of the guilty: if Jesus allows himself to be
led to the Passion like the "lamb led to the slaughter" of
Isaiah 53, or even like the "emissary goat" on the great Day
of Atonement (Lev 16), it is not without a secret accord of
his consciousness and will, finally finding its source in the
trinitarian decision of redemption.[29] The "only-begotten"
Son (Jn 1:18) of the Father was in fact aware of the unique
character of his Person and the universal character of his
mission. By that von Balthasar rediscovers, but through the
subjective experience of Jesus, the objective meaning that,
following Saint Paul (2 Cor 5:14–15) and the ancient Roman liturgy, tradition has always given to the Cross: that of
a *sacrum commercium*, of a wonderful exchange between the
one who has the power and authority to die for all and those
whom this fact mysteriously affects, procuring justification
and filial adoption for them through grace.

[29] On this decisive point, which it is impossible to explain here, refer to
Theo-Drama, vol. 3: *The Dramatis Personae: The Person in Christ*, trans. Graham
Harrison (San Francisco: Ignatius Press, 1992), pp. 187–88. On the limits
of the theory about the emissary goats proposed by R. Girard in his first
publications, *La Violence et le sacré* (Paris, 1972) and *Des Choses cachées depuis
la fondation du monde* (Paris, 1978), refer to the critical review by Father von
Balthasar published in *Communio* 5/3 (1980): 73–75. Since then, the author
has published numerous works in the same line: from *Le Bouc émissaire* (Paris,
1982) to the most recent books: *Je vois Satan tomber comme l'éclair* (Paris, 1999)
and *Celui par qui le scandale arrive* (Paris, 2001).

3

MERIT, SUBSTITUTION, SACRIFICE OF THE CHURCH

Scripture is content to affirm the objective fact of the *pro nobis*. With respect to the way in which the latter is accomplished, it observes a respectful silence, for substitution is, in the end, a mystery whose ultimate elucidation is impossible. Nevertheless, common experience can provide certain elements that are useful for understanding it. In Saint Thomas, it is in the end around the notion of merit, but of supereminent merit, that the exposition of the salvific action is articulated: for the properly human action of Christ, particularly in the Passion, is that of a Divine Person who, through his Incarnation, has been constituted by God, in view of his universal propitiatory mission, "Head of the whole Church" and, insofar as they are his members, of all men of good will.

What does this notion mean more precisely? Is it capable of explaining adequately the mysterious exchange of which the Second Letter to the Corinthians speaks?

It is from the very nature of human action that Aquinas deduces the general moral notion of merit, which finds its place in the context of retributive justice, where each is recompensed according to his actions. Of itself, merit is not reward, but that by which one tends toward that reward: it is the human action insofar as it is morally good and, because of its qualities, possesses the dignity of an adequate reward. It has its "principle" in the one who posits it, "inwardly", "in the soul", and its "root" in the "charity" that animates it.[1] The relationship of justice that merit presupposes is nevertheless a person-to-person relationship: one that works justice and one that benefits from it.[2]

With regard to God, this interpersonal relation is actually what permits us to speak of a merit of justice, for between the act posited by man and the obtaining of eternal life, there cannot exist, in the strict sense, any proportional equality. If there is merit in the presence of God, it is because of an order of justice that God himself established with respect to his creatures and that, for this reason and this reason only, confers on the latter a certain right to beatitude, which is the end for which they were created. Of itself, such a beatitude completely transcends what man can achieve by his own means; it is the free and gracious gift from one person, God, to another person, man, whom God also makes capable of acting freely in view of that beatitude.

This principle of collaboration is at the heart of the Thomist theology of grace: in the meritorious act, God acts in us through the infusion of his grace; far from substituting himself for man, grace arouses in him the collaboration of his free will, so that he participates actively, through his consent to God, in his own justification and filial adoption.

How are we to interpret the salvific efficacy of the Passion in the light of this doctrine? Christ, the eternal Word of the Father, could not, of course, merit what belongs to him by right, the fullness of personal grace (cf. Jn 1:14).

---

[1] *S. Th.* III, 19, 3, and 48, 1; cf. 49, 6 ad 1. To explain the two interconnected aspects of merit, Saint Thomas (I-II, 55, 1 ad 3) uses the image of running.

[2] *S. Th.* II-II, 58, 2.

— But as man, through his mortal body and his soul subject to suffering, he participates fully in our condition as pilgrims, *in potentia ad plenitudinem*,[3] and thus in expectation of the exaltation in glory. In him, the possibility of merit is inscribed in the perfection of his human nature, endowed with its own will and operation. It is thus appropriate for him to receive, by his merits, the reward for his action: the exaltation and glory of his body. Merits thus acquired, the instrument, indispensable in its order, is the voluntary and free operation of the Christ-Man who, through obedience and love, hands himself over to the power of death according to the sovereign plan of the Father. The principal source, however, is nonetheless the habitual grace—distinct from the grace of union that he possesses by virtue of his divine nature—that is proper to the soul assumed by the Word at the moment of the Incarnation. Now that grace, Saint Thomas specifies, is not only personal, it is a "capital" grace.

— By the notion of sanctifying grace, we generally mean the motion permitting Christians to reach eternal life through a merit of strict justice (*meritum condigni*). In the case of the Christ-Man, that grace is not limited, as with them, to his own life; it is communicated to others: the actions of Jesus are ordered to universal salvation. God, in his merciful economy, has constituted him in fact Head of the Church and author of the salvation of all men. Just as he established Adam the principle of all nature, so he established Christ the principle of the grace that is destined to all as members of his Body.[4] In fact, just as in man, the action of the head belongs to the whole body, so the activity of Christ is the source of merit for all mankind. Because of the superiority of the grace that is proper to him as Head, all those who are

[3] *Super Epistolam ad Philippenses*, ad Ph 2, 7, lect. 2, no. 57.
[4] *S. Th.* I-II, 114, 6, and III, 19, 4.

united to him as his members and constitute with him one single mystical person, benefiting from his salvific activity.

> Christ received grace, not only as an individual, but also as Head of the Church, so that the grace might overflow onto his members. That is why the works of Christ have the same effects for himself and his members as the actions of a man in the state of grace have for himself. Now it is obvious that any man in the state of grace who suffers for justice thereby merits his salvation, according to the words of Saint Matthew: "Blessed are those who suffer persecution for the sake of justice." Consequently, by his Passion, Christ has merited salvation not only for himself but also for all his members.[5]

Farther on, Saint Thomas again explains how, incorporated in Christ as the members are to their head, we receive the effects of the merits of his Passion:

> By the Passion that he endured through obedience and through love, Christ delivered us from our sins, we who are his members, his Passion being the price of our redemption. It is as if a man redeemed himself from a sin he had committed with his feet by means of a meritorious work he did with his hand. For, just as the natural body is one, constituted by different members, so the whole Church, the Mystical Body of Christ, is considered a single person with its Head, which is Christ.[6]

In order to be effectively saved, however, men must open themselves freely to the work of their salvation, must unite themselves to Christ who has suffered for them, and must, as members of the Body, receive from their Head, through

[5] *S. Th.* III, 48, 1. The same principle is presented with respect to satisfaction: III, 48, 2 ad 1.
[6] *S. Th.* III, 49, 1.

faith and the sacraments of faith proposed by the Church, the spirit of divine filiation that renders them capable of meriting, with their glorified Lord, the immortal glory of their body.

∾

For our modern mentality, which has to a large extent lost the sense of social corporeity and, on the contrary, acquired an acute sense of inalienable individual liberty, such a doctrine of supereminent merit remains somewhat abstract and in any case takes into account too little of historical reality to appear altogether convincing. The question that von Balthasar addresses to it from the existential view that is his own is of knowing if it explains in a satisfactory way the exchange worked at the Cross, where a single person, the unique Son of the Father, takes on himself the punishment of death that sin brought to all, in order that mercy might be shown to all and that the eternal life obtained through his Passion, his death, and his Resurrection might be offered to all.

The question finds a particularly eloquent crystallization in the discussion of 2 Corinthians 5:21, whose Thomist exegesis we have presented above.

According to the Catholic explanation still accepted today, Saint Paul intends to signify by this that God has, as it were, identified Christ with sin by making the punishment due for sin fall on him in order to deliver us from it. Likewise, this interpretation says, if Christ "has become a curse for us" (Gal 3:13), it is in the sense that he united himself with the curse that weighed on sinful man. In any case, an exchange in the strict sense between the sinless Son of God and sinful man does not seem possible. Would not admitting

this lead to attributing to Christ the fact of being a sinner?[7]
On the other hand, for the modern mentality, the extrinsicism of the reparation in relation to the fault to be expiated
hardly provides a satisfactory argument in favor of the *pro
nobis*. If the "capital" relationship of Christ to the members
of his Body does not imply a kind of identification, is sin
really assumed, are sinners truly actualized in him?

Of course we can speak of "sacrifice", in his regard, only
by way of analogy: applied to Christ, the notion of sacrifice
no longer has anything to do with the meaning, familiar in
the history of religions and still, in a certain way, in the Old
Testament, of an action intended to appease a wrathful God
. . . as if God could experience anger in the way men are
subject to the passions!

By handing over his own Son for us, the Father manifests
his love for the world (Jn 3:16; cf. Rom 8:32). By letting
himself be handed over into the hands of sinners (Mt 17:22
par.) as the sacrificial lamb (Jn 1:29) who expiates their sins
(Rom 3:25), Jesus acts in his own right, in an inner consent that authorizes the author of the Letter to the Hebrews
to see in him the priest of the sacrifice (Heb 4:14–15; cf.
Jn 10:17–18). Moreover, the Swiss theologian prefers to
the term sacrifice (*Opfer*) that of abandonment to the end
(*Hingabe, Dahingabe*), which connotes a love that can go all
the way to letting himself be outraged, violated by sin, but
also, inseparably, a love that exposes itself voluntarily, in the
name of sinners, to the fire of divine anger.

With the intention of better expressing the intrinsic character of the exchange between the Innocent one and sinners, von Balthasar proposes the notion of substitution (*Stell-
vertretung*), which to him signifies a true exchange of place

[7] Cf. Luther, *WA* 8, p. 86.

(*Platztausch*), in accordance with the thought of Saint Paul: "Christ . . . though he was rich, yet for your sake he became poor, so that by his poverty you might become rich" (2 Cor 8:9). The term suggests the gesture of someone who takes something upon himself in order to be able to remove it from the other.

By taking up the poverty, the curse, the deficiency from which sinners suffer, Christ opens up the space, prepares the place that can be occupied by these others for whom he substitutes himself, and he does so in order that the latter may find within themselves the riches, the life they are lacking. The Crucified ransoms us by suffering something "in our place", that is, in the place that reverts to us sinners, in that place of total separation from God where those go through their revolt against the Creator. In his flesh, our sin is "condemned" (Rom 8:34), our alienation is "broken down" (Eph 2:14), and that even before we were able to express an assent to it: "while we were yet sinners" (Rom 5:8). Which means, comments our theologian, that the Paschal event causes a kind of ontological transfer of place: through the Cross, God "has delivered us from the dominion of darkness and transferred us to the kingdom of his beloved Son, in whom we have redemption, the forgiveness of sins" (Col 1:13–14); "one man's act of righteousness", in fact, objectively, "leads to acquittal and life for all men" (Rom 5:18).

On the basis of this first substitution, accomplished through pure grace, will man himself then, in his turn, be able to expiate, annihilate his sin or, in Saint Thomas' words, merit his salvation or even at least collaborate in his redemption? In other words, does the essential moment of exclusivity that the *pro nobis* possesses in the first place comprise secondarily a certain inclusivity on behalf of men, saved by grace?

Saint Paul, who freely exemplifies it through his own life

as a convert, suggests it in this way: "Now I rejoice in my sufferings for your sake, and in my flesh I complete what is lacking in Christ's afflictions for the sake of his body, that is, the Church" (Col 1:24). Or again, "Even if I am to be poured as a libation upon the sacrificial offering of your faith, I am glad and rejoice" (Phil 2:17). The grace of salvation, obtained without merit, stimulates the Christian to take part in the active fruitfulness of the Cross. The redemption is exclusively the work of Christ, but it includes at the same time the possibility of a "work" on the part of Christians reconciled with God. This is shown by one page from von Balthasar that is a model of doctrinal and spiritual equilibrium:

> One *can* recall here that it would not conform to the authentic human solidarity of Jesus were he to carry through his work of salvation in an exclusive fashion, shutting out all others, or, more exactly, that it would be inhuman not to draw within the exclusivity which befits him as the only Son of God a moment of inclusivity. There *must* therefore, a priori, be a certain taking up of the Old Testament theology of expiatory suffering and of martyrdom into Christology. It is in this sense that we should interpret the logion which grants to the disciples the capacity to drink the cup and undergo his baptism (Mark 10:38ff.). However, one would do better to let this "assumption" first disappear into the mystery of Christ so as to understand the making space on the Cross as the sovereignly free grace of the New Testament.[8]

Nothing needs to be added to the suffering of Jesus, if by that we mean that something was lacking in it as such. If the Church provides something additional, it is only on top of the foundation of Christ's Passion. We could say that the latter has made satisfaction for all the sins of humanity so well that he has reserved for his own the possibility of

---

[8] Von Balthasar, *Mysterium Paschale*, pp. 135–36.

collaborating, "through him, with him, and in him", not only in their own salvation but in the salvation of their brothers. Adrienne von Speyr suggests that those who thus accompany him on the way of the Cross bring him a kind of consolation.[9]

We understand, consequently, von Balthasar's motive, in the present volume, for adding to his study on "Christ the Redeemer" a conference presenting "Mary and the Church in the Redemption". Forgoing the idea of treating this theme as it deserves,[10] we will close this postscript with a few explanations about the "sacrifice of the Mass" to which the theologian alludes at the beginning of the second conference.

That, in the eucharistic celebration, the faithful ask Christ to take them up into his abandonment of love to the Father and to men is now an almost uncontested truth, even among many Protestants;[11] what is debated today is whether they themselves actively offer a sacrifice.

The debate has shifted to that other question: Does the sacrifice of Christ remain, in the last instance, outside their person, or, in the eucharistic celebration, the assembly of the

---

[9] Cf. *Nachlasswerke*, vol. 8 (Einsiedeln, 1975), p. 21; cf. *Nachlasswerke*, vol. 3 (Einsiedeln, 1966), pp. 200–202. On the participation of Mary in the work of the Redemption, see her first book: *Handmaid of the Lord*, trans. E. A. Nelson (San Francisco: Ignatius Press, 1985), pp. 37–40, and particularly the more complex work: *Mary in the Redemption*, introduction by H. U. von Balthasar, trans. Helena M. Tomko (San Francisco: Ignatius Press, 2003).

[10] A few preliminary reflections on the subject can be found in my article "Mary's Role in the Incarnation", in *Communio: International Catholic Review* 30/1 (2003): 5–25.

[11] In *Creator Spirit* (trans. Brian McNeil, C.R.V., Explorations in Theology, vol. 3 [San Francisco: Ignatius Press, 1993], pp. 188–89), von Balthasar refers in this regard to the study of P. Brunner, *Leiturgia* 1:358. On the general theme of the Eucharist, in French, from a catechetical point of view: *L'Eucharistie, don de l'amour* (Chiry-Ourscamp, 1994).

Church, as a subject distinct from Christ, is their person associated with the act of that sacrifice itself? And if we accept that we see in the Mass a sacrifice of the Church, what is the relation between the absolute *prius* of the solitary work of the Cross and its "mysteric" worship? At the Last Supper, Jesus anticipates in sacramental form the free offering of his life; he has no need of the historical experience of the Cross in order to live already in a real manner, at that moment, the efficacy of his love "to the end" (Jn 13:1). Can one now apply to the Church what is affirmed with respect to Christ and speak of the Eucharist as a "*sacrifice* [which is also kenotic] *of the Church*"?

According to classical theology, "the Mass is an unbloody 'renewal' of the sacrifice of the Cross. It is the same sacrifice, but 'sacramentally'."[12] The Augustinian theology of the infrangible unity between the Head and the Body (cf. Eph 4:15; Col 1:18) helps to explain this sacramental character: "Sacrament of the sacrifice of the Head, the Mass is the sacrament of the sacrifice of his members."[13] In the Eucharist, the Church participates in the spiritual attitude and action of the Redeemer: "He willed that there be a daily sacrament of this reality, the sacrifice of the Church, which, being the Body of which he is the Head, learns to offer herself through him."[14] But where, then, is the identity of the sacrifice between the Head and the Body realized? In the instrumental cause of the ministerial

---

[12] Y. de Montcheuil, *Mélanges théologiques* (Paris, 1946), p. 54.

[13] A. Hamman, article "Euchariste" in *DSp* 4:1582. Cf. Saint Augustine, *Sermo* 227: ". . . nos ipsos voluit esse sacrificium suum, quod demonstratum est ubi impositum est primum illud sacrificium Dei et nos—id est signum rei—quod sumus" (*Opere* 32/1, p. 388).

[14] ". . . Cuius rei sacramentum cotidianum esse voluit Ecclesiae sacrificium, quae cum ipsius capitis corpus sit, se ipsam per ipsum discit offerre", Saint Augustine, *City of God*, X, 20.

priesthood, in pure functional obedience? It does not seem so, for the priest only opens the space to Christ, who is the principal agent. Or must we go farther and maintain, with O. Casel and the Marialaach school, that the sacrifice of the Head becomes the sacrifice of the Church not only through the priestly service but through the more personal participation of the Church and of her sacrifice united to that of Christ?[15]

In his essay in response to this essential question, von Balthasar strives to take into consideration the various linked and distinct factors indicated by Scripture. The participation of the Body in the sacrifice of Christ that is the foundation for the common priesthood (cf. 1 Pet 2:5, 9; Rev 1:6) is justified only on the basis of faith in his unique sacrifice. In that sacrifice, accomplished "for you", "for our sins" (1 Cor 11:24; 15:3), the faithful one is first of all in a position of receptivity. If we become the active subjects of it, it is only insofar as we were taken up into him when we were still "enemies" (cf. Rom 5:8). The *opus operantis* of the faithful presupposes the work of Christ, who enjoys, as we recalled above, an absolute anteriority. The objectivity of the redemption is manifested in the sacrament of baptism as the Church understood it and practiced it very early on with regard to children: as *opus operatum*. However, the theolo-

---

[15] "The whole *Ecclesia*, the holy assembly, is the subject of the divine liturgy. . . . Within the structure of the Church, each member of this Mystical Body collaborates in a real way in the worship of the whole, each according to his position. . . . It is truly the whole Church, and not the clergy alone, that must take active part in the liturgy. . . . Through the sacramental character of baptism and confirmation, *each* of the faithful participates in the priesthood of Christ. . . . In order for this participation to reach its perfection, the faithful must actualize their objective priesthood and live it by sharing in a personal way in the mystery. . . . The Head and the members are united and are but one in offering the sacrifice to the Father" (O. Casel, *Le Mystère du culte dans le christianisme* [Paris, 1946], pp. 96–100).

gian specifies, following Adrienne von Speyr, the baptismal regeneration in question[16] does not take effect without the participation of Mary-Church. At the foot of the Cross, the Mother pronounces in the name of all believers an unconditional Yes to the sacrifice of her Son.[17] An element that is jointly constitutive of the sacrifice of the Cross, this Yes is not placed on the same level as the Yes of Christ, whose work remains absolutely transcendent: it is, in its order, a Yes to that work itself, the active (sorrowful) acceptance of an event that the faithful Bride allows to happen without being able to intervene except by uniting herself to it with all her heart. It constitutes, in this sense, the archetype of all ecclesial faith. By lovingly associating itself with the offering of the Head, the Body becomes "one body"[18] with him on Golgotha. In that way, von Balthasar recalls once again the Augustinian idea of the complete sacrifice of the total Christ, *Caput et membra*,[19] but with greater emphasis on the nuptial dimension. The universal priesthood of the faith-

[16] Cf. James 1:18; 1 Pet 1:3, 23; Jn 3:3–8; 1 Jn 3:9.

[17] H. Urs von Balthasar, *Theo-Drama*, vol. 4, *The Action*, trans. Graham Harrison (San Francisco: Ignatius Press, 1994), pp. 395–98. The *opus operatum*, the work accomplished in the soul of the subject who has received the sacrament of baptism, is certainly the result of the *opus operantis*, the action of the minister, but it is possible only through an original communication of the divine life. According to Saint John, the latter happened at the Cross, where Christ and Mary-Church, his Bride, engendered the "son", and with him potentially all the faithful.

[18] 1 Cor 6:15–16.

[19] "This whole redeemed City, which is to say, the society of the saints, is offered to God as a universal sacrifice by the High Priest who, in the form of a slave, went to the point of offering himself for us in his Passion in order to make of us the Body of so great a Head. It is in fact this form that he offered, it was in it that he offered himself, because it was thanks to it that he is Mediator, in it that he is priest, in it that he is sacrifice. . . . Such is the sacrifice of Christians: the many are but one body in Christ. And the Church never ceases to reproduce this sacrifice in the Sacrament of the altar,

ful finds its realization in the relation of Christ and Mary-Church accomplished on the Cross, there where the New Adam, united to the New Eve, offers himself as a holocaust and becomes at one and the same time "sacerdos, offerens, et oblatio".[20] On its nature and its specific efficacy, Father Jean Daniélou had some very profound reflections. "God", he said, among other things, in a spiritual conference to those he was directing, "will never be loved more than by Christ, which is to say, by humanity clothed by the Word, on the Cross. Thus we cannot offer more to God than this infinite love with which Christ loved him; that is the whole meaning of the sacrifice of the Mass."[21]

If it is a proper action of the Church—and Scripture affirms this by recalling the Lord's instruction: "Do this in memory of me" (1 Cor 11:25)—it is in virtue of her personal conformation, in the Passion, to the Redeemer's obedience of love. The offering of the faithful acquires its value only because of the loving abandonment of the "Woman" (Jn 19:26) to the unique, unrepeatable, definitive sacrifice of the "Man" (Jn 1:30), into which this offering is incorporated. Let us note, nevertheless, that this essentially feminine action of the Church will never be able to attain in existential perfection the immaculate Yes of Mary.

In the Church here below, an unresolved tension remains between objective holiness (of the *opus operatum*) and subjective holiness (of the *opus operantis*). Such a tension did not exist at all in Christ, since he realized in himself, from the beginning, the perfect unity of minister and love; nor did it

---

well known to the faithful, where it is shown that she herself is offered in what she offers", Saint Augustine, *The City of God*, X, 6.

[20] "In this way he is priest: it is he himself who offers, and he is himself the oblation", Saint Augustine, *The City of God*, X, 20.

[21] J. Daniélou, *Contemplation, croissance de l'Église* (Paris, 1977), p. 99.

at all exist in the Mother of God, who, at the foot of the Cross, is totally united to the sacrifice of her Son. Christ loved the Father with an infinite love. For the Church in pilgrimage on earth, to unite herself to her offering necessarily means obeying the instruction that he imparted to the disciples in the course of his active life before entering into his Passion. The hierarchical Church cannot put herself in the place of Jesus, but she is authorized to carry out ministerially the commandment she received from him. From the day of his Resurrection, Christ has drawn the faithful every day into his sacrifice, and in that way this sacrifice remains a real and living presence: in the Offertory and the Consecration of the Mass, Christians offer this sacrifice; in Communion they are offered with him, intimately associated to him by the power of the Holy Spirit who acts in them, objectively (through the sacred ministry of the apostles: Jn 20:22; Acts 1:8) as well as subjectively (in their own heart: Rom 5:5).

In brief, for von Balthasar, the Eucharist is, in the first place, the sacrament of Mary-Church that, since the Cross, has been united to the definitive offering of Christ to the Father on behalf of men and that, in conformity to the instructions at the Last Supper, actualizes his sacrifice not only on the objective level, in virtue of the power conferred by the sacrament of orders, but on the subjective level, in virtue of the holiness, communicated and lived, of Christian life.

Between the mystery of salvation, accomplished on the Cross, and its eschatological realization in the "members of his Body" (Eph 5:30), the Eucharist exercises its intermediary function of actual presence with a fullness whose efficacy is made manifest in a real way by the pilgrim Church, in a distance that remains until he comes (cf. Rev 22:20).

JACQUES SERVAIS, S.J.